W9-BXL-774

The Basis of
Millennial Faith

The Basis of
Millennial Faith

by

The REVEREND FLOYD E. HAMILTON, Th.M.

author of

"The Basis of Christian Faith"
"The Basis of Evolutionary Faith"
"The Reformed Faith in the Modern World"

WM. B. EERDMANS PUBLISHING COMPANY
Grand Rapids   1955   Michigan

THE BASIS OF MILLENNIAL FAITH
by THE REV. FLOYD E. HAMILTON, TH.M.

———————

Copyright, 1942, by
Wm. B. Eerdmans Publishing Co.

All rights in this book are reserved. No part may be reproduced
in any manner without permission in writing from the publisher,
except brief quotations used in connection with a review in a
magazine or newspaper.

Set up and printed, July, 1942
Third printing, January, 1955

PREFACE

This book is the result of many years of study of the problems connected with the prophecies about our Lord's Second Coming. When the writer first became a Christian, and for a number of years afterward, he was a premillennialist, because that and postmillennialism were the only explanations of prophecy with which he was familiar, and postmillennialism seemed to be contradicted by many of the statements of Scripture about the condition of the world when Christ comes again. Believing, therefore, that there were only two views of eschatology from which to choose, the writer accepted premillennialism as the theory which most nearly squared with what the Bible taught about the condition of the world when the end of this age comes.

During the last year in Seminary, however, the view which is now known as amillennialism came to the writer's attention, and the fact was brought home forcibly that instead of only two views of prophecy, there were three views from which to choose, and that the third view avoided not only the difficulties of postmillennialism but also the difficulties in the premillennial view of which he had gradually become aware.

During twenty years on the mission field, the writer lived in a foreign mission station whose members were almost all premillennialists, and a great many discussions over the problems of eschatology crystallized the solutions of those problems that acceptance of the amillennial view provided. It was possible to work in peace and harmony with the premillennialists, however, because our view of the task of the Christian church in this present age, and of the condition of the world before Christ comes, coincided with the premillennial view.

After hearing a talk by a noted premillennial Bible teacher who was visiting the mission field a number of years ago, the writer asked the Bible teacher whether she was familiar with the amillennial view of prophecy, and the reply was in the negative. The conviction grew on the writer, from that experience, that a great many premillennialists had never heard of amillennialism or had heard only a distorted version of its beliefs. This might cause little harm were it not for the fact that in recent years there has been an increasing tendency on the part of some premillennial leaders, to regard amillennialism as a heresy, and to refuse cooperation in the churches with believers in amillennialism. Such a situation is indeed unfortunate. The historic position of the Christian Church has been that no official pronouncement should be made by the church as a church on the millennial issue, and that members were to be allowed to hold any view they desired. That is the wise course for all Christians to follow in the fight against Modernism and the anti-Christian paganism of this modern civilization. When Christ comes again we will know who is right on these questions, so why fight over the order of the eschatological events connected with that return of Christ? Especially is that true when both parties believe that the world will not be converted *before* Christ comes again. If our task now is to preach the gospel and to witness to an unbelieving world of the unsearchable riches of Christ, trusting in the Holy Spirit's power to add to the church those who are being saved, then we should be able to carry on that task in harmony no matter what our view of eschatology may be. In the hope that many premillennialists may be brought to an understanding of what amillennialists believe, and so be brought to realize that hearty cooperation with them in the church is possible, this little book is being written.

FLOYD E. HAMILTON.

Los Angeles, Cal.
June, 1942

TABLE OF CONTENTS

The Basis of
Millennial Faith

Chapter I

THE BLESSED HOPE

"LOOKING for the blessed hope and appearing of the glory of the great God and our Saviour Jesus Christ" (Titus 2:13).

From New Testament times to the present, the Church of Christ has been a hopeful church. Pessimism has no place in the Christian consciousness. No matter how dark the days or how discouraging the outlook on the world, Christians, who understand the teaching of the Word of God, and believe it to be true, have universally been optimists. Optimists, not because they believed that man was becoming better and better and making the world constantly a better place in which to live, or because they shut their eyes to the evils that surrounded them in the world, but because they knew the God in whom they trusted, and knew that His promises can never fail of fulfilment.

When Jesus Christ was received up into heaven, and a cloud hid Him from the eyes of the little group of disciples on the Mount of Olives, as they stood gazing up into heaven, two angels stood beside them in the form of men in white, and told them that "this Jesus, who was received up from you into heaven, shall so come in like manner as ye beheld Him going into heaven" (Acts 1:11). Since He left them in a visible form, He will come again in a visible form. Since He left them in a cloud, undoubtedly the same cloud that filled the Holy of Holies in the temple during the period when God manifested His presence in the temple at Jerusalem, called the "Shekinah" glory of God in Hebrew, so He will come again in His own time, in the same Shekinah glory of God, in appearance like a cloud. Since he left as the one to whom "All power is given on earth and in heaven" (cf. Matt. 28:18), He will return in the same powerful way, "rendering vengeance to them that know not God, and to them that obey not the gospel of our Lord Jesus, who shall suffer punishment, even eternal destruction from the face of the Lord and from the glory of His might, when he shall come to be glorified in His saints, and to be marvelled at in all them that believed" (II Thes. 1:8-10).

It is the appearance of our Lord Jesus Christ in the Shekinah glory that is the "blessed hope" of the church. Not the "secret rapture" of the church; not the setting up of an earthly "millennial kingdom" in which the Jews have the preeminent part; but rather, as Paul puts it in Titus 2:14, which we quoted in the first paragraph, the appearing of the Shekinah glory and our Lord and Saviour Jesus Christ in a visible form, just as He went into heaven. That is what the church is waiting for, longing for, and hoping for. That is what causes the church of Christ to be optimistic in the midst of discouragements, dangers and disappointments.

A patient who comes to the surgeon for an operation does not love the pain, nor look forward to the weeks of suffering on his bed in the hospital with pleasure, but he can be cheerful and optimistic in spite of them because he knows that the surgeon has promised him health at the end of the experience of pain. The mother on her bed of travail does not enjoy the pain, but the hope of the birth of a son enables her to endure the suffering that must precede it. It is the "blessed hope" of the appearing once more of the departed "Shekinah" glory of God, and the visible appearing of Christ in the midst of the Shekinah glory, that has enabled the church of Christ to be undiscouraged when it has fallen into evil times, and it looks to the eyes of the "world" as though it has seen its better days and is rapidly approaching complete eclipse. The Christian knows that the Lord Himself has promised that the "gates of Hades shall not prevail against" the church (Matt. 16:18). The Christian knows that things will probably get worse before the "blessed hope" is realized, for Jude, the brother of the Lord, said, "In the last time there shall be mockers, walking after their own ungodly lusts"

(Jude 18), while Peter said, "that in the last days mockers shall come with mockery, walking after their own lusts, and saying, Where is the promise of His coming? for, from the day that the fathers fell asleep, all things continue as they were from the beginning of creation" (II Pet. 3:3-4). Paul said that before Christ comes there will be a falling away from the faith and the revealing of the man of sin, the incarnate spirit of the anti-Christ who "opposeth and exalteth himself against all that is called God" (II Thes. 2:4), whom Christ Himself will "slay with the breath of his mouth, and bring to nought by the manifestation of his coming" (II Thes. 2:8). "But the Spirit saith expressly, that in later times some shall fall away from the faith, giving heed to seducing spirits" (I Tim. 4:1). The Christian reads the words of our Lord in Matt. 24, and is not at all disturbed when he looks at a world gone mad with war, knowing that our Lord Himself prophesied those very things: "And ye shall hear of wars and rumors of wars; see that ye be not troubled: for these things must needs come to pass; but the end is not yet. For nation shall rise against nation, and kingdom against kingdom; and there shall be famines and earthquakes in divers places. But all these things are the beginning of travail. Then shall they deliver you up unto tribulation, and shall kill you, and ye shall be hated of all nations for my name's sake. And then shall many stumble, and shall deliver up one another, and shall hate one another. And many false prophets shall arise, and shall lead many astray. And because iniquity shall be multiplied, the love of the many shall wax cold" (Matt. 24:6-12).

The Christian looks at the world today with Christianity being persecuted and true Christianity in Japan, that refuses to give the glory that belongs to God alone, to the alleged sun goddess, almost exterminated; with true Christianity hounded to death in the war-ridden nations of Europe; with Modernism almost triumphant in the great churches of America and the British Empire; with Bible believers everywhere looked down upon, ridiculed, and subjected to petty persecution; the Christian sees all these things but instead of being discouraged and downhearted, experiences a new surge of hope that perhaps the time when the "blessed hope" is to be realized, is almost upon us.

But why is the "appearing of the glory of the great God and our Saviour Jesus Christ," the "blessed hope" of the church? Well, in the first place, the Word of God makes it perfectly plain that that appearing of Christ marks the destruction of all the powers of evil in the world. When He comes again, no longer will it be true that Right will be "forever on the scaffold, Wrong forever on the throne!" The Hitlers of the world will all be overthrown. Injustice and tyranny will vanish as mist before the morning sun. Those who have put their trust in Jehovah, who have believed in Christ as their Saviour, will be vindicated before the eyes of a terrified world. Sin and evil will be finally swept away by the wrath of the living God, as are straws before the hurricane. Then shall the "righteous shine forth as the sun in the kingdom of their Father" (Matt. 13:43). No more will Satan and his hosts deceive the nations; no more will they be able to entice the children of God into sin, and no more will suffering and sorrow be the lot of God's elect.

But in the second place, not only will sin and sinful habits be left behind when Christ comes in glory; there will be a blessed reunion of the redeemed at the feet of the Saviour. Those who are alive will again be united with loved ones who have fallen asleep in Christ. Parents will again see the children whom they loved before God took them home to Him. Orphaned children who have put their trust in their Saviour, will be reunited to Godly parents who have gone to be with their Lord. Husbands and wives whom death has separated will again look into each other's eyes, when we are all gathered before the throne. What a time of rejoicing that will be! The redeemed of the Lord will meet the saints and apostles and prophets who have been with their Saviour through the centuries, and will enjoy the fellowship to which all of God's people look forward with hope and longing.

But more precious than even this thought is the fact that we will be "clothed upon" with our glorified bodies, when we are made perfect in holiness. "We that are alive, that are left unto the coming of the Lord . . . shall all be changed, in a moment, in the twinkling of an eye, at the last trump: for the trumpet shall sound, and the dead shall be raised incorruptible, and we shall be changed. For this corruptible must put on incorruption, and this mortal shall have put on immortality" (I Thes. 4:15 and I Cor. 15:51-54). No more will we have sickness and death. No more will we experience the temptations of the flesh. No more will we know the disgust and self-reproaches that have followed defeats before the assaults of Satan. Sin and deformity, pain and death will all be left behind and we will shine forth in glory before the glorious presence of our Saviour and Redeemer.

But this is not all. The creation itself "also shall be delivered from the bondage of corruption into the liberty of the glory of the children of God" (Rom. 8:21). "The heavens shall pass away with a great noise, and the elements shall be dissolved with fervent heat, and the earth and the works that are therein shall be burned up. . . . But according to His promise, we look for new heavens and a new earth wherein dwelleth righteousness" (II Pet. 3:10 and 13). It will indeed be a changed earth, a new earth, after the fire of God's wrath has burned out all sin and evil, and the new Jerusalem has come down out of heaven, "made ready as a bride adorned for her husband" (Rev. 21:2). The glorious future to which we look forward after the "appearing of the glory" and the Second Coming of our Saviour, will have a heavenly and earthly counterpart. Everything will be perfect, with no sin and death ever again to be present therein. But best of all, the coming again of the Shekinah glory of God will symbolize the constant presence of the manifest glory of God Himself openly revealed to all men on earth and in heaven. Again God will walk with man as He did in the Garden of Eden before the fall. Restoration of man to complete and perfect communion with God, directly and visibly under God's control and government is the real meaning of the coming again of the Shekinah glory of God. Immanuel, God with us, is the most precious meaning of the "Blessed Hope".

The Christian Church has indeed differed as to the interpretation of the prophecies relating to the order of events preceding and following the Second Coming of Christ, but as to the fact of His Coming again there has been universal agreement among those who accept the Bible as the Word of God. Because of this unity of belief in regard to the Second Coming, and because there has apparently been room for sincere difference of opinion as to the way in which the prophecies concerning it are to be interpreted, the church has almost universally refused to make such interpretations articles of the creeds of the various churches. In other words, almost all evangelical branches of the Christian church have left the individual Christian free to accept his own interpretation of prophecies concerning the Second Coming of Christ, and receive all those who believe in the *fact* of the Second Coming, as Christian brethren.

A development in recent years in this respect is to be regretted. In some circles acceptance of a particular interpretation of these prophecies has been made the criterion of orthodoxy. Those who believe just as thoroughly in the Bible as the Word of God, and to whom the "Blessed Hope" of the appearing of the "glory of the Great God and our Saviour Jesus Christ" is just as precious as it is to those who hold the opposite interpretation of the prophecies relating to the Second Coming, are nevertheless refused acceptance as Christian brethren, or at least discriminated against in such Christian circles. Not all those who hold to the interpretation of the prophecies which goes under the name of "premillennialism," are guilty of such discrimination against those who hold the view of prophetic truth called "amillennialism," but a sufficiently large section of them do so discriminate, to warrant the attempt to justify the view in question, according to sound exegetical canons of Biblical interpretation. If this unreasonable prejudice against amillennialism could be removed from the minds of these premillennialists, this book would be well worth while.

In the present situation it is indeed strange that certain sections of the premillennialists do so endeavor to ostracize amillennialists.

Advocates of both views earnestly hope for the fulfillment of the prophecies regarding the "Blessed Hope". Advocates of both views alike look for the *imminent* return of Christ as soon as the relevent prophecies are fulfilled. Advocates of both views do not expect the world to be all converted through the preaching of the Gospel in this dispensation, so that both expect Christ to come at a time when it might readily seem to an unbeliever that Christianity was defeated. Advocates of both views therefore agree as to the duty of Christians and the program of the Christian church up to the time when Christ comes in the clouds and the elect Christians are raptured to meet Him in the air. We will *then* know who is right on these questions, anyway, so why quarrel now about points in regard to which there may be honest differences of opinion, but which ought not to be points to cause division among Christian brethren? Why cannot advocates of both views, in brotherly love, examine the Word of God objectively without prejudice, to see "whether these things be so"? If they differed as to what the task of the Christian church is in the present age, or differed as to the methods to be used in the present desperate fight against Modernism and Neo-paganism, one could understand the opposition to amillennialism by some premillennialists, but when we are both engaged in a struggle to the death against these forces of iniquity, at such a time when we ought to be united, the continued opposition to amillennialism by these premillennialists, seems puerile and futile. I would not for a moment imply that the questions at issue between them are unimportant, for questions of truth or error are always important, but they are questions which are not vital either to life or conduct as Christian believers, and therefore, since they have no direct relationship to salvation, they should be questions to be examined objectively, in the privacy of the study, by friendly discussion and unprejudiced exegesis, rather than made the subject of quarrels, or tests of orthodoxy.

Ignorance of what an opponent actually teaches too often is the cause of opposition, and it is because the writer has heard the amillennialist teachings distorted and misinterpreted by well-meaning but misguided premillennialists, that the present book is written to "give an account of the faith that is in us," and if possible to show that amillennialists do not have the "horns" with which they are too often credited. If some premillennialists may be led to see that the millennial issue is not completely closed, but that there is room for sincere difference of opinion between those who hold equally to the belief in the Bible as the Word of God, this book will not have been written in vain.

Chapter II

PREMILLENNIALISM

The General Theory.

IN order to get a clear idea of what this is all about, the various interpretations of the prophecies will first of all be given with no attempt to show the grounds for the views held by the various schools of thought. Premillennialism is the view that when Christ comes he will set up an earthly kingdom in which Christ is the king, and certain classes of believers are to reign with Him on the earth, over the nations. The nations will bow before the stern "iron rod rule" of Christ, though they remain unconverted and rebellious at heart. After a thousand year reign, Satan, who was bound at the beginning of the millennium, is to be loosed to deceive the nations for a time and to gather them in rebellion against Christ. Their hosts are to be destroyed by fire from heaven. The resurrection of the wicked dead is then to take place, and the judgment of the great white throne (Rev. 20:11-15) takes place. The righteous dead are said to have been raised before the beginning of the millennium and to have been raptured at that time to meet the Lord in the air. This in brief is the outline of the general theory called premillennialism. There is great difference of opinion between the different varieties of premillennialism as to most of the other features of the general prophetic picture, so these widely different views must now be described.

Historic Premillennialism.

There have been many premillennialists in the past who have held to the view which we will call "historic premillennialism."

The most noted of these advocates according to Alexander Reese, in "The Approaching Advent of Christ," are Irenæus, Justin Martyr, Tertullian, in the ancient Christian church, Mede and Bengel, and in more modern times, Alford, Andrews, David Baron, Birks, Bonar, Ellicott, W. J. Erdman, Gordon, Guinness, Kellogg, Moorehead, George Muller, Maitland, B. W. Newton, Ryle, Saphir, Stifler, Tregelles, Trench, and West. In Germany, and the Continent, Auberlen, Bleek, Christlieb, Delitzsch, De Wette, Ebrard, Ewald, Godet, Hofman, Lange, Van Oosterzee and Zahn are the most noted expounders of the theory. The view which this imposing array of scholars and theologians have advocated is as follows:

1.   Preceding the Second Coming of Christ the Antichrist will gather his followers for a great assault on the church of Christ. For some time he appears to be practically victorious, and institutes a great tribulation for the church, which passes through the tribulation.

2.   At the close of this tribulation period Christ is suddenly seen appearing on the clouds of heaven, the dead in Christ rise first, the living elect are transfigured and the people of Israel look on Him whom they have pierced, repent and are saved, and the whole elect people of God are then raptured to meet the Lord in the air.

3.   Christ then descends to the earth with His Bride, the Church, destroys the Antichrist and at the judgment of the Sheep and Goats, separates the righteous from the unrighteous, condemning the latter to eternal punishment.

4.   Christ then sets up His millennial kingdom, ruling over the nations with a rod of iron, after the binding of Satan at the beginning of the millennium.

5.   At the close of the millennium Satan is loosed from his prisonhouse, gathers the nations, in numbers as the sands of the seas, to war against the saints, but they are destroyed by fire from heaven.

6. Then follows the resurrection of the wicked, and the great White Throne Judgment (Rev. 20:11-15).

7. This in turn is followed by the new heaven and the new earth (Rev. 21), and the setting up of the eternal kingdom of God.

Even among these who hold to the "historic premillennialism," there is little agreement as to many details of the theory. Some hold that the millennial kingdom will be predominantly Jewish, with Christian Gentiles in a rather subordinate place, while others hold that the martyrs, and those who worshipped not the beast nor his image nor had his mark upon their forehead and hand, will occupy the ruling place during the millennium. Others believe that the Jews reign as unconverted Israelites during a restoration of the Jewish kingdom of Palestine, under a theocracy, with the church in heaven. Others hold that the whole church of Christ will reign during the millennium, with no distinction between Jews and Gentiles. There is a great deal of confusion as to the place of the restored temple worship during the millennium, while the premillennialists in general experience much difficulty in reconciling Old Testament eschatological prophecies with New Testament prophecies concerning the Second Coming. There is also much confusion as to the relationship between the transfigured saints with spiritual bodies, and the untransfigured "nations" over whom Christ reigns, during the millennium.

Pre-Tribulationists.

About a hundred years ago a man named J. N. Darby, founded a group of Christians who have become known as "The Brethren," or "Plymouth Brethren." His followers, Wm. Kelly, W. Trotter, and C. H. M., were the pioneers of the movement, but in more recent times W. E. Blackstone, in "Jesus is Coming," F. W. Grant, James M. Gray, A. C. Gaebelein, F. C. Ottman, and particularly C. I. Scofield, the author of the "Scofield Reference Bible," have popularized what we may call a new view of the events preceding and following the Coming of Christ. It is important to note that there is a vast difference between the teachings of these men and the teachings of the old historic premillennialists.

1. Instead of one Second Coming of Christ, there are two distinct stages, so that in reality we should speak of the Second and Third Comings of Christ.[1] The Second Coming will concern the church alone, and will occur at the beginning of the Seventieth week of Daniel 9:24-27, when Christ comes for His church. The Third Coming will concern Israel and the world, and occurs at the close of the Seventieth Week, when Christ comes *with* his church. Between the Second and Third Comings of Christ there will be at least seven years, the Seventieth Week of Daniel 9:24-27.

2. At the Second Coming of Christ the Righteous dead of New Testament times with the Righteous dead of the Old Testament, and the living Church of Christ, will be transfigured, after the first resurrection, and raptured to be with Christ during the seven years, where they receive rewards at the Marriage Feast of the Lamb.[2] (Most of this group hold that the Rapture will be a *Secret* Rapture,[3] while this group again breaks up into those who believe that only those who are *looking* for the Second Coming will be raptured, while other Christians who are not looking for it will be left behind to go through the Great Tribulation.[4] The other group hold that all Christians who are in the Church of Christ will be raptured at that time.)

3. After the rapture of the church, the Antichrist sets up his kingdom, and institutes the Great Tribulation.[5] The church which has already been raptured, therefore, will not pass through the Great Tribulation.[5]

4. The Holy Spirit is removed from the world at the time of the Second Coming.[6] (This is called the *Coming* of Christ, while the Third Coming in glory is called the *Day,* the *Revelation* or the *Appearing* of Christ. This distinction between the terms is usually emphasized by this group.) After the Second Coming, the Jews return to Palestine, mostly in unbelief. However, there is a small *Remnant*[8] who remain faithful to the true God, though they do not

---

1 These references in the text refer to the "Notes" at the close of the book, pp. 147 ff.

accept the saving work of Christ.[9] During the latter part of the week they preach the *Gospel of the Kingdom* far and wide according to the Great Commission of Matthew 28:19. An immense number of the inhabitants of the world believe this *Gospel of the Kingdom*,[10] and pass through the Great Tribulation, though they are not yet true believers or a part of the true Church of Christ.[11]

5. At the close of the seven years there will be another resurrection of the martyred saints of the tribulation period, though these resurrected saints will not be connected with the Church of God.[11]

6. At the close of the seven year period the Antichrist gathers his hosts against the Remnant and those Gentile believers who have not been martyred, at the Battle of Armageddon (Rev. 16:16). Christ then comes in glory *with* the church, holds the Sheep and Goat judgment, (the basis of which is how the nations have treated the Jews, who are the "brethren" of the Lord, the separation thus being on the basis of good works).[12] The living Remnant, and the Gentile "nations," then enter the Millennial Kingdom set up by Christ, but with unglorified bodies.[13]

7. At the Third Coming of Christ Jews who remain in unbelief after their brethren have believed the preaching of the witnesses, "look on Him whom they have pierced," believe and are saved (all while the Holy Spirit is absent from the world!), and then enter into the millennial kingdom of Christ with unglorified bodies.[14]

8. The millennial kingdom is set up with the Jews in the chief authority, [15] with the temple and its worship again established in Jerusalem.[16] The believing Jews and the "nations" who are ruled over with "the rod of iron," still have natural bodies, but sin is sternly repressed, and though the nations are rebellious at heart, they are forced to bow the knee to Christ who rules from Jerusalem.

9. Satan was of course bound at the close of the seven year period, but at the end of the millennium he is loosed from his prison, gathers the rebellious nations to war against the saints, and these nations are destroyed by fire from heaven. This is followed by the resurrection of the wicked, the Great White Throne Judgment and the setting up of the eternal kingdom of God.

10. During the millennium it is not quite clear what the relationship of the Church is to the unglorified believers in the earth. Most probably would say that their real home is in heaven but that they could visit the millennial kingdom at will.[17] Some would doubtless say that the church will join in the millennial reign of Christ.

It is seen at a glance that this whole scheme is totally different from that of the old historic premillennialism. This is not the place to enter into a criticism of the view, but we call attention especially to the fact that since the Holy Spirit is said to be withdrawn at the beginning of the Seven Years, any who believe *after* that time could not be Born Again of the Spirit, but would believe in their *own* strength. This directly contradicts the Bible teaching that men are dead in sin and incapable of doing anything righteous unless the Holy Spirit gives them the New Birth. We also at this time call attention to the preaching of the Gospel of the Kingdom by the semi-Christian Remnant during the Tribulation period. This is *not* the Gospel of salvation through believing in the atoning work of Christ, so it must be "another gospel" and come under the condemnation of which Paul speaks in Gal. 1:8.

Ultra-dispensationalists.

There are many variations of the Pre-Tribulation theory, but there is one group of whom we wish particularly to speak. Though the members of the group will probably resent the name, we will call them the Ultra-dispensationalists. All Christians distinguish between at least three dispensations: (1) The dispensation of works, before the fall of man, when man was placed under a covenant according to which obedience to God's command would bring eternal life, while disobedience brought eternal death to themselves and to their descendants except as God's grace brought redemption. (2) The Old Testament dispensation up to the coming of Christ, during which salvation was limited to God's chosen race and to those who were brought into the Covenant People. Throughout this whole period salvation was by grace through faith in God and His promises of redemption through the Messiah, imperfect though the believer's knowledge of the way of salvation may have been. Implicit trust in God was the way by which God bestowed salvation upon believers. The covenant of circumcision was instituted as the seal of the believer's faith in God. The law of Moses was instituted to teach the hopelessness of trying to earn salvation by good works and obedience to the law, and so, by increasing the transgressions, to reveal to man his lost condition and lead him to rest implicitly in the promised Redeemer. At the same time it gave man a standard by which to measure his sinful heart, and a rule of life for those who lived by faith. (3) The third dispensation is the New Testament dispensation, under which salvation is by faith in Christ for those who are mentally responsible and of God's chosen people, both Jews and Gentiles. Throughout both the dispensations after the fall of man, salvation was *only* by grace through faith in God and His promised Redeemer. There is thus a unity in the Zion of God throughout the whole period from Adam to the present. The Old Testament saints and the New Testament saints are all part of the same church of God throughout the ages. Nor will there be any other basis of salvation at any time in the future, except through belief in the redemption that is in Christ Jesus. There have been several covenants, but no change in the way of salvation.

Dr. C. I. Scofield, in his "Scofield Reference Bible," page five, lists seven dispensations. They are the dispensations of innocency, conscience, human government, promise, law, grace and kingdom.

The first lasted up to the fall of man, the second down to the Covenant with Noah, the third down to Abraham, the fourth, that of promise, from Abraham to the Mosaic Law, which was the fifth dispensation lasting up to Calvary. The sixth is the present dispensation, which will last up to the millennial kingdom, the last of the dispensations. Such a division might in itself be unobjectional were it not for the fact that Dr. Scofield declares that each dispensation represented a different way in which God tested man's obedience. The greatest objection to the scheme, however lies in the fact that Dr. Scofield claims that, during the dispensation of promise, Abraham and his descendants were under a covenant of grace as heirs to the promises given to Abraham, but that at Sinai, Israel *rashly* accepted the law in place of the covenant of promise! This put law in place of grace! From that time on they forfeited the estate of grace and lived in the state of law! Grace again came into the picture at Calvary, while in the kingdom in the future, law again will take the place of grace.

Now this teaching that under the law men did righteously and so *became* righteous, while under grace they are *declared* to be righteous for the sake of Christ's righteousness which is clothed upon them, raises the question at once as to how the Old Testament saints were saved. The notes of Dr. Scofield would necessitate declaring that they were saved by keeping the law. Fortunately Dr. Scofield is not consistent on this point for he elsewhere declares that grace is the only way of salvation. However, the position taken sets the dispensation of law squarely over against the dispensation of grace, and so contradicts one of the central teachings of the Bible.

As a corollary of this disjunction between law and grace, the ultra-dispensationalists declare that the primary application of certain parts of Scripture is to the people of different dispensations. Thus the Sermon on the Mount and the Lord's Prayer are said to be not primarily for the people of this age, the church age, but for the kingdom age. The epistles are the parts of the Bible which concern the church age, the age of grace. Some even go so far as to say that only the Pastoral Epistles particularly concern the people of this age. Others declare that the Gospels, particularly the Gospel of Matthew, do not primarily concern us, while all of them would declare that since we are now under grace and not under law, we need not trouble ourselves with the ten commandments!

The effect of such teaching is of course to lead Christians to think that it is unnecessary for them to keep the Lord's Day holy. In Korea it was used by some Korean Christians as an excuse for bowing at shrines dedicated to the sun goddess, the mythical ancestress of the Japanese emperor, even though they admit that it breaks both the first and second commandments. Few would go so far as to claim that they have liberty to break the sixth and seventh commandments, though the position taken would seem to allow even that.

It is perfectly true that we are not under law but grace. No one would claim that we are today saved by keeping the law perfectly. That does not mean, however, that we are free today from the demands of law, or that it is not our life rule or guide. Christ said that if we loved Him we would keep His commandments, not in order to earn our salvation, but simply because we love Him and therefore try to please Him by keeping His commandments. Our union with Christ by faith means that we live the new life of law-keeping as an expression of our love for Him who gave Himself on the cross to die for us. Thus the law, while not regarded as the means of salvation through obedience to its demands, becomes the constant goal and standard by which Christians measure their love for their Redeemer.

Premillennialists of all varieties almost universally teach that the millennium will be the earthly reign from Jerusalem as capital, of the Messiah, over the Gentile nations who are forced into outward obedience to His "iron rod rule."[18] These nations will, at the close of the millennium when Satan is loosed, rise in rebellion against Christ, because they have been wicked at heart. Most premillennialists say that the Jews will have chief place in the millennial kingdom after restoration to Palestine.[19] They are said to be in their natural bodies capable of dying and giving birth, though they are presumably believers in Christ's redemptive work. Other premillennialists hold that the glorified church with spiritual bodies will reign with Christ over the nations.[20]

Chapter III

POSTMILLENNIALISM

THE second theory of eschatological events is called post-millennialism, because it teaches that a thousand years of peace and righteousness will precede the Second Coming of Christ. The postmillennialist looks for the conversion of practically the whole world through the preaching of the Gospel in this dispensation. Then, with the establishment of justice and righteousness throughout the world, with the elimination of war and evil, the world will enter into the Golden Age when righteousness shall cover the earth as the waters cover the sea and every knee shall bow and every tongue confess Jesus as Lord and Saviour. They expect the world to become better and better, until at last truly Christian government is established all over the world, the hosts of Satan are defeated, and Satan himself vanquished from the earth.

As a part of the universal reign of righteousness the teaching of the New Testament that the Jews will be converted to Christianity, (Rom. 11:26), follows as a logical corollary. The postmillennialists deny that there will be any national restoration of the Jews as a nation in Palestine.* All that the New Testament teaches is that the Jews will be saved, not that they will again become a separate nation.

Postmillennialists do not dwell much on the question of the binding and loosing of Satan, mentioned in the 20th chapter of the Revelation. What is to occur would be purely figurative, referring to the limiting of Satan's power through the triumphs of

---

* The establishment of the nation of Israel with so little orthodox Judaism connected with it, shows that this new nation is not to be considered as the fulfilment of prophecy.

Christ and the Gospel ushering in the millennium preceding the coming of Christ. They would declare that it is quite possible that at the close of the 1000 years of peace there might be a flare up of Satanic power to be destroyed by the appearance of Christ on the clouds in glory.

They hold that when the prophecies of the end time are fulfilled, at the sound of the trumpet, all the dead, both saved and unsaved, will be raised, while the righteous will be raptured with glorified bodies of living believers, to meet the Lord in the air during the battle of Armageddon. After the welcome, the vials of God's wrath will be poured out on the earth, destroying the wicked, overturning the armies of the Antichrist at the conclusion of the battle of Armageddon, (which begins just before the coming of Christ in the clouds), and Christ will judge the earth in the judgment of the Great White Throne. This judgment will be the same as the judgment of the sheep and the goats, and the judgment scene of II Thes. 1:7-10.

After the final judgment, Christ turns over the kingdom to the Father, and the eternal kingdom of Christ will be established. The new heavens and earth will come into existence with the coming to earth of the new Jerusalem pictured in Rev. 21-22.

The plausibility of the whole postmillennial theory lies in what would seem to be the intrinsic probability of ultimate victory through the preaching of the gospel to the whole world. Since God has placed the spreading of the gospel in the hands of Christians, and since through 1900 years the gospel has indeed spread throughout the world so that there are believers in almost every land, it would seem logical to conclude that the same process will continue until all the world is evangelized and Christianized. Unquestionably there has been great progress in the raising of moral and ethical standards throughout the world, so that Christendom in the past has come to dominate the thinking of peoples individually and nationally. This would seem to indicate that the same process will continue until evil is completely vanquished from the earth through the processes now at work in the world.

The events of the last forty years, however, have revealed the fallacy in such reasoning. World War No. I, shattered the hopes of the advocates of peace through international cooperation, in the Hague Peace Congress. The failure of the League of Nations and the breaking of World War No. II, gave the final death blow to any hopes of the ushering in of an era of universal peace and joy through the interplay of forces now in action in the world. Indeed it is strange that such an idea could ever have arisen from a study of the teachings of the New Testament. The doctrine of election itself, teaching as it does the selection of some to salvation out of a group of unregenerate men, would inevitably indicate that the forces of Satan will continue to exist in the world throughout the inter-adventual period. The belief that all will become righteous would seem to contradict the plain teaching of election, that some are saved and others lost.

Moreover the teaching of the parable of the wheat and the tares, Matt. 13, that both the sons of the kingdom and the sons of the evil one are to be in the world right up to the end of the age, clearly contradicts any view of the universality of Christianity throughout the world for a thousand years. The various passages which on the surface would seem to indicate the contrary, such as the parable of the mustard seed and the parable of the leaven, are capable of the interpretation that they refer only to the completion of the number of the elect, rather than indicating that they refer to the whole world. The Book of the Revelation, itself, is so full of the pictures of evil on the earth at the time of the coming of Christ, that it is difficult to see how anyone can escape the force of the teaching that both good and evil will continue up to the time of the Second Coming. Christ's teaching that there will be a great tribulation preceding His coming, that the Antichrist will gather his forces against the church, that there will be a great apostasy in the church itself, and that it will be hard to find faith on the earth when He returns to earth all so clearly indicate the unconverted condition of the world at the time of the Second Coming, that it is hard to see how believers in the Bible as the Word of

God can continue to hold that there is to be a universal reign of righteousness preceding the coming of Christ. Christ prophesied the continuation of wars up to the time of his coming again, and this in itself would indicate the futility of trying to banish them by human agreement when the hearts of myriads of men will continue evil.

Premillennialism has gained much of its plausibility through its pointing out these facts concerning Scripture and human nature, while postmillennialism gained much of its plausibility through pointing out the inconsistencies in the premillennial position and the errors of its teaching about the events to follow the coming of Christ in the clouds. The facts of Scripture would seem to indicate that two tendencies will be present in the world up to the time of the Second Coming of Christ. First, the number of the elect will continue to be gathered into the church, thus increasing steadily the total number of the saved until that number is completed. Second, the forces of evil will grow worse and worse in the world, as Satan in his madness uses every power at his command to overthrow the church of Christ. This battle or war between the right and the wrong will grow in intensity and power until it culminates in the great tribulation under the Antichrist, and the battle of Armageddon. Then will Christ come in the clouds. The premillennial theory is therefore right in what it asserts of the condition of the world up to the time of the Rapture, while the postmillennialists are right in what they assert concerning the events to follow the Rapture.

Chapter IV

AMILLENNIALISM

THE third generic view of the interpretation of the facts of
Scripture relating to eschatology, is called *Amillennialism.*
The name itself is unfortunate in that it would seem to indicate
that its advocates do not believe in the thousand year period of
Revelation 20. The name literally means "no millennium," while
as a matter of fact its advocates believe that the millennium is a
spiritual or heavenly millennium, rather than the earthly one of a
literal reign of Christ on earth before the final judgment. From
one point of view it might be called a variety of postmillennialism,
since it believes that the spiritual or heavenly millennium *precedes*
the Second Coming of Christ. The only mention in the Bible of a
kingdom of Christ limited to a 1000 years is in the 20th chapter
of the Revelation where it is said that the "souls" are seen reigning
with Christ during the 1000 years. The amillennialist interprets
this as indicating the spiritual reign with Christ of the disembodied
spirits in heaven, during the 1000 years. A thousand, the number
of perfection or completion, is held to be the symbolic reference
to the perfect period, or the complete period between the two
comings of Christ.

The picture of eschatological events, without any discussion at
present of the supporting Scripture passages, is as follows. Like
the premillennialist we view the world as a mixture of good and
evil up to the time of the Rapture. We have no hope or expecta-
tion that the whole world will grow better and better until it is all
converted to Christianity. We expect that wars will continue

right up to the time of the end when Christ comes to set things right. We expect the elect to be gathered out of an evil world, though we do believe that the command of Christ to preach the gospel to the whole world must be obeyed, and that it is our duty to endeavor to establish a Christian society as far as it is in our power to do so, but while we have the obligation to do this, we by no means expect that the whole of society will be Christianized. In fact, we expect the forces of evil to grow more and more violent in their opposition to Christianity and Christians. This in no way excuses us from the attempt to propagate Christian principles as well as the gospel in the world.

At the close of the present age we expect the forces of evil to head up in a powerful combination of political, economic and religious power led by the Antichrist. At the close of the reign of the Antichrist or Man of Sin, he institutes a terrible persecution against the Christian Church (not against the Jews as some premillennialists assert). In this terrible tribulation vast numbers of Christians are killed, but at the climax, when the hosts of Satan seem to be on the point of complete victory, during the battle of Armageddon, Christ appears in the Shekinah glory, the resurrection of all men takes place, and the transfigured bodies of the dead and living saints are caught up to welcome their Saviour. Then, as a terrible out-pouring of the wrath of God occurs, smiting the unbelieving nations of the world into destruction, the living Jewish people look "on Him whom they pierced," repent and believe instantaneously in their Messiah. Simultaneously with their conversion and regeneration by the Holy Spirit, as they see Christ coming on the clouds, they too are transfigured with the living Church of Christ, and join in the rapture of the united body of the elect church of Christ of the ages. This completes the number of the elect, and from that point onward there is no more salvation for men.

As soon as the rapture is consummated, Christ and His Church return to earth for the Great White Throne Judgment, or, since the descriptions of the Judgment in the Bible do not *necessitate* believing that it occurs on the earth, perhaps this judgment occurs in the air after the rapture. It is not clear from Scripture as to what happens to the resurrected bodies of the wicked. Certainly they are revivified if not transfigured, and since they gather instantaneously after their resurrection before the Great White Throne, for the final Judgment, and since eternal punishment concerns the soul rather than the body of man, there is reason to believe that the resurrected bodies of the wicked have superhuman qualities, though they certainly are still sinful bodies, filled with corruption and evil, marred by the deformities of sin. At any rate they "hear the voice of the Son of Man and live," at the same time as the righteous dead.

After the Judgment, the eternal kingdom of God is established in the new heaven and on the new earth, for the old heaven and the old earth are passed away. The chief characteristics of the new heaven and the new earth will be the absence of sin and evil, the eternal manifestation of the presence of the Triune God before the eyes of the Redeemed, and the perfection of the glorious new earth. This will continue through all eternity.

In the above descriptions we have not attempted to present the Scriptural basis for the views held, but have simply tried to present a unified picture of the views as a whole, for the sake of comparison. Since all of the various points presented are concerned with highly controversial subjects, it is not expected that the premillennial reader will offhand accept the amillennial views here set forth without evidence. The only reason for presenting them in this way is for the sake of contrast, that there may be a clearer understanding of the evidence as it is presented in the following chapters.

Chapter V

MUST WE INTERPRET OLD TESTAMENT PROPHECIES LITERALLY?

ONE of the principal teachings of premillennialism is that the prophecies of the Old Testament must be interpreted literally unless the language of the Bible clearly indicates that a figure of speech is used by the author. Since the Old Testament contains definite promises of certain blessings to Israelites, it is claimed that those literal blessings must be given to the racial Israelites and to them alone, regardless of their rejection of Christ as Saviour.[21] Since the Messiah is promised a reign upon the throne of David, it is held that the throne of David will again be established in Jerusalem, and all the nations of the world will go up to Jerusalem to worship, during a thousand year millennial kingdom. In the same way all the eschatological passages of the Old Testament which were not fulfilled at the time of Christ's first coming, are to be literally fulfilled in the future, after His Second Coming, according to premillennial principles.

Now we must frankly admit that a literal interpretation of the Old Testament prophecies gives us just such a picture of an earthly reign of the Messiah as the premillennialist pictures. That was the kind of a Messianic kingdom that the Jews of the time of Christ were looking for, on the basis of a literal interpretation of the Old Testament promises. That was the kind of a kingdom that the Sadducees were talking about when they ridiculed the idea of the resurrection of the body, drawing from our Lord the clearest statement of the characteristics of the future age, that we have in the New Testament, when He told them that they erred "not knowing the Scriptures nor the power of God " (Matt. 22: 29). Of course it is true that the Apocalyptic literature of the period preceding the birth of Christ had added many imaginary features to the Jewish ideas of the kingdom, and though the Jews set no thousand year limit to the kingdom, they took the whole idea from a literal interpretation of the Old Testament prophecies. In fact, the Jews were looking for just such a kingdom as that expected by those premillennialists who speak of the Jews holding a preeminent place in an earthly Jewish kingdom to be set up by the Messiah in Jerusalem. Jesus Himself, in speaking of that whole idea said, "The kingdom of God is within (or in the midst of) you" (Luke 17:21), thus contradicting the idea that it was to be an earthly, literal, Jewish kingdom.

Let us look for a moment at the various features of this kingdom which come from a literal interpretation of the Old Testament prophecies. Israel is to be restored to Palestine; other nations exist elsewhere but they are subservient to the Jews, (Is. 60:1-22) ; people will have mortal bodies, live in houses, eat of physical vineyards, bear children, be subject to sickness and death, though not to the same degree as at present, (Zech. 14) ; the temple and the temple service will be restored with bloody sacrifices as sin-offerings to make atonement for the people, (Ezek 45:17) ; the temple priests will teach the people the difference between clean and unclean things; the tribes of the earth will come up to Jerusalem yearly to keep the feast of the tabernacles. To this picture obtained from a literal interpretation of the Old Testament prophecies, the premillennialists add that while the Messiah will reign in righteousness and every knee will bow to Him and confess Him as Lord, the nations of Gentiles will, in the main, be rebellious at heart, so that Christ reigns over them with a rod of iron, until they all rebel at the close of the millennium. This is the picture of a physical, earthly kingdom which a literal interpretation of all the prophecies of the Old Testament gives. The premillennialist insists that if we do not believe in this picture of the future, we reject the "plain teaching of Scripture," and are guilty of distorting the Word of God.

At first sight, to one who accepts the Bible as the Word of God and the only infallible rule of faith and practise, the argument of the premillennialist seems unanswerable. However, a little deeper study of the implications of the position taken raises a doubt in one's mind in regard to the necessity of interpreting *all* Old Testament prophecies literally, and if it be admitted that even *one* prophecy is to be interpreted symbolically or spiritually, the whole principle of interpretation used by the premillennialist breaks down, and other principles of interpretation must be admitted possible. It then becomes a question as to *how* we are to apply the other principles of interpretation.

In the first place, for Christians to look forward to a literal temple in Jerusalem, with the restoration of the whole sacrificial system, seems to dishonor the sacrifice of Christ on the cross. Premillennialists insist that these sacrifices will be memorial sacrifices pointing back to the cross of Christ, but not only does the Bible say nothing about such memorials; *any* memorials are unnecessary when the one to be memorialized is present in person, as Christ would be after His Second Coming. The very heart of evangelical truth is the once-for-all character of the sacrifice of Christ on the cross of Calvary, in place of believers, so that to reinstitute the animal sacrifices as a memorial would tend to focus the saints' attention upon the type rather than upon the antitype, the glorified Lord! In Hebrews 9:24-28 we are told that "Christ now at the end of the ages hath been manifested to put away sin by the sacrifice of Himself." His sacrifice is permanent, complete, and never to be repeated, according to the writer of the Epistle to the Hebrews. "Christ . . . through His own blood, entered in once for all into the holy place, having obtained *eternal* redemption " (Heb. 9:12). Does it not clearly follow from the finished work of Christ that there is now no necessity for any types or symbols of the old temple worship to be repeated in the future?

Christ's redemption was final, definite, complete and never to be repeated. To return to the old system of animal sacrifices after He returns in glory, would be to return to the "weak and beggarly elements whereunto ye desire to be in bondage over again " (Gal. 4:9). Yet if the literal method of interpretation of all Old Testament prophecies is to be followed, this is exactly what will be necessary. The last chapters of Ezekiel give us a picture of the restored temple, with animal sacrifices again to be offered. This is a picture upon which even premillennialists do not like to dwell, for they appreciate quite well the fact that the restoration of animal sacrifices would seem to dishonor the once-for-all character of Christ's sacrifice. In Dr. Scofield's Bible there is only one comment on these last eight chapters of Ezekiel in which he claims that these offerings will be memorial, looking back at the cross, (Scofield's Bible, p. 890).

Now consider for a moment the incongruity of the idea that all the blood and filth, and, no matter how careful the attendants might be to cleanse the place each day, the stench of the slaughter-house, should be again instituted in a future temple which would be the very center of all worship throughout the world! It would be like using the flickering candle as a memorial for the light of the sun, when the sun in all its glory has risen! To claim that these sacrifices would be offered as a "memorial" of the cross, when the blessed, crucified, risen and glorified Saviour was Himself present in person, would seem to dishonor Christ and to approach dangerously close to blasphemy of His person. In the old dispensation animal sacrifices were necessary to point believers to the necessity of a substitute to bear the penalty due to them for sin. But after Christ cried "It is finished," while hanging on the cross, that whole system of types and shadows was done away with, and the "sun of righteousness rose with healing in his wings," once for all. The rending of the temple veil from top to bottom signified that the way was opened for every believer directly into the presence of God Himself. Every believer now has his sin covered with the blood of Christ's sacrifice, and recognizes that Christ is His eternal substitute. In the future state, even were there a millennium, what possible need could there be for a "memorial," either of Christ or His cross, with Christ present in person before the eyes of the believer? Not only would there be no need of such a thing; it would be a positive hindrance and stumbling block to the proper worship of Christ! The constant danger of all such aids to worship as the Roman Catholic uses in his ceremonial worship, such as images, crucifixes, rosaries and elaborate ritual, is that the worshipper will concentrate his attention on the symbols and forget to worship the Lord Himself. That would be exactly the danger of such a reinstituted memorial temple worship and ritual: it would tend to take the minds of the worshippers off our blessed Lord, and fix them on the "beggarly elements," bringing them again under the bondage of the law!

But there is a still greater objection to interpreting the last eight chapters of Ezekiel literally, and referring them to the period following the return of Christ. It is a fundamental principle of premillennialism that Christ is to set up an earthly millennial kingdom in Jerusalem with Himself as the theocratic king. If that should be true we would have the strange spectacle (Ezek. 46:2) of the "prince" entering the temple by the way of the eastern gate, standing by the post of the gate, *while the priests prepare his burnt offering and peace offering!* What a spectacle! To imagine for a moment that human priests could offer *sacrifices* for the Prince of Peace, the sinless Saviour, who by sacrifice of Himself forever put an end to all sacrifice! As though God the Son needed to offer sacrifices for Himself!

We must dwell still further upon this incongruous spectacle, in order to emphasize the hopeless maze of difficulties into which a literal interpretation of *all* the Old Testament prophecies plunges us. According to a literal interpretation of Ezekiel 40-48 the whole ceremonial law is to be again set up in Israel. There will be meal-offerings, trespass-offerings, peace-offerings, sin-offerings, as well as burnt-offerings (Ezek. 42:13; 45:17). The passover and the feast of unleavened bread will again be celebrated (Ezek. 45:21-22). The priests will have to observe the elaborate ritual of changing their robes before and after ministering in the temple holy place, "that they sanctify not the people with their garments" (Ezek. 44:19). The whole precious doctrine of the individual priesthood of believers will apparently have to be discarded then, for only the priests can approach and enter the holy place in the temple before the Holy of Holies, where God's Shekinah glory dwells (Ezek. 42:14). The priests are forbidden to marry widows except widows of other priests, and cannot defile themselves by approaching dead persons other than near relatives (Ezek. 44:22, 25). One of the principal duties of the priests will be to teach the "people the difference between the holy and the common, and cause them to discern between the unclean and the clean" (Ezek. 44:23). But most important of all these features of the ceremonial law, is the *requirement of circumcision* for those who are to enter the sanctuary. "No foreigner, uncircumcised in heart and *uncircumcized in flesh,* shall enter into my sanctuary, of any foreigners that are among the children of Israel"! (Ezek. 44:9). This would throw into the discard Paul's Epistle to the Galatians, for that was written specifically against those Judaizers who insisted that it was necessary to be circumcized as well as to believe in Christ for salvation. Just what would our premillennial friends suggest that circumcision would be a "memorial" of? Is it not plain that the principle of literal interpretation of *all* Old Testament prophecies is reduced to an absurdity by the mere contemplation of such a prospect during the alleged millennium? Christ Himself provided the true memorial of His death, in the Lord's Supper, and that was to be observed only "till He come," when the need for a memorial would be done away, and it, together with all other "former things have passed away" (Rev. 21:4).

But if the premillennialist admits that we are not to expect *all* these prophetic details, including even circumcision, to be fulfilled during the millennium, then the whole argument for the literal fulfillment of all Old Testament prophecies must be abandoned, for there is nothing to indicate that these last eight chapters in Ezekiel are figures of speech. However, if it is admitted that there is a possible symbolic interpretation for even a few of these passages, then certainly the same principle of interpretation can be used for other similarly difficult prophecies.

But what, it may be asked, is the amillennial interpretation of these chapters in Ezekiel? Well, we would first of all point out that there has never yet been any temple that corresponded to the one described in Ezekiel. Neither Ezra's temple nor Herod's temple in any way can be identified with it, so there is no way of claiming that the prophecy about it has *already* been literally fulfilled. We have already pointed out the absurdity of supposing that it will be *literally* fulfilled in the future. That shuts the believer in the inspiration of Ezekiel up to only one possible explanation of these prophetic pictures. These last chapters of Ezekiel must be intended to teach *spiritual truths under the symbolism of the temple and the restored nation!* Let it be remembered that the whole Israelitish nation represented God's ideal relationship to mankind, marred though it was with abuses and sin and disobedience. The whole history of Israel taught the spiritual lessons of God's demands upon man, the theocratic relationship of God's people to God, and the failure of the whole plan because of sin and disobedience.

Now then, in the last chapters of Ezekiel particularly we have the picture of what the ideal relationship of God's people to God ought to be. In other words, we have here a symbolic picture of the proper relationship of the true, invisible Kingdom of God on earth to the Sovereign God, as it ought to manifest itself in human government and society. Since in the Old Testament dispensation before the coming of Christ the only way which God had revealed by which man could approach God was through the ritualism of the temple, with the whole sacrificial system typifying the redemption of Christ, naturally this prophetic picture presents the worship of God through the temple ritual, as the ideal mode of worship. The spiritual truths here taught are, (1) The worship of God is to be supreme over the whole of society, (represented in Ezekiel by the city), human government, (represented in Ezekiel by the prince), ecclesiastical organization (represented by the priests and Levites), and over the individuals themselves. The Sovereignty of God should be the very *center* of human life and thought and action. (2) When any phase of human society is *not* so subvervient to God, the "times are out of joint," and terrible abuses creep in. When the national government is supreme over the church, civilization, and the individual, we have the tyranny of ancient Rome and modern Russia. When the ecclesiastical organization is supreme over the government and secular civilization, we have abuses like those under the Church of Rome, in the Middle Ages and in Catholic countries to-day where the church controls the government. When civilization dominates the other realms we have conditions such as exist in the materialistic, worldly life of England, France and America. Every one of these situations represents terrible abuses, and violates the fundamental ideal of the Kingdom of God described under symbolic language in the last chapters of Ezekiel. The ideal condition is that there described, when the government, the church, and civilization, with its arts and sciences and human individuals, all stand on equal footing under the recognized and practised worship of the Sovereign God, who is supreme over every realm and whose supremacy is recognized in every realm of life. The sinful nature of man has consistently prevented the realization of this blueprint of the Kingdom of God on earth, yet all the while, if men would only understand and follow the guideposts God has here provided, we have before us the plan according to which all the ills of human life could be remedied. Thank God this ideal relationship *will* be realized in the eternal Kingdom of God which will follow the return of Christ in glory. Not that we are to expect any of the details themselves given in Ezekiel to be literally fulfilled, but that the *truths* represented by those details will be realized in the new heaven and the new earth.

But there is another, equally serious objection to the insistence on the necessity of a literal fulfillment of every Old Testament prophecy. Such a literal interpretation of the Old Testament prophecies brings them into *direct conflict with the New Testament prophecies* pertaining to the events preceding and following the Second Coming of Christ. We have pointed out that the Old Testament gives us a picture of the Jews restored to their own land, with the capital in Jerusalem, and all the nations of the earth coming to Jerusalem to worship the Messiah during His earthly reign from Jerusalem. Men are to have mortal bodies, bear children, eat the fruit of vineyards, grow sick and die — a thoroughly human, earthly picture. The New Testament description of the future age following the return of Christ is in direct contradiction to such a state. Jesus Christ gave a vivid picture of the condition of things during the period following what premillennialists call the "first resurrection" or the "out-resurrection." (Premillennialists usually insist that the Greek words "ek nekron," "from the dead," always mean the resurrection of the righteous dead from among the total number of the dead. The wicked dead are not to be raised, according to the premillennialist, until after the 1000 years of the millennium. The term "ek nekron," "from the dead," or "out-resurrection," therefore, always refers to the period following this "first" resurrection.)

In Luke 20:27-36 (cf. Matt. 22:23-30; Mark 12:18-27) the Sadducees, who denied any resurrection from the dead, were ridiculing the idea of the resurrection period current among the Pharisees of that time, (that is, the idea that the Jews would be resurrected and take part in a Messianic kingdom with Jerusalem as a center). They cited the case of the woman, undoubtedly a Jewish woman, who had seven husbands, and asked whose wife she would be in the resurrection. Jesus answered: "The sons of this age marry and are given in marriage; but they that are accounted worthy to attain to that age, and the resurrection (ek nekron) from the dead, neither marry nor are given in marriage; for neither can they die any more; for they are equal to the angels, and are sons of God, being sons of the resurrection." The literal interpretation of the Old Testament prophecies demands that men shall marry, have children, be sick and die during the period following the resurrection. Jesus says they will *not* marry, and of course therefore *not* bear children, and will *not* die during that same period following the resurrection! Jesus' statement is in *direct contradiction* to the Jewish idea of the Messianic kingdom and likewise to the premillennial idea of the kingdom, derived from the literal interpretation of the Old Testament prophecies. In the parallel passage in Matt. 22:29 Jesus told the Jews: "Ye do err not knowing the Scriptures nor the power of God"! In other words, their literal interpretation of the Old Testament passages caused them to err, and shows that they did not know the Scriptures. Is that not an indication that the present day literal interpreters of the Old Testament prophecies also "err not knowing the Scriptures"?

Now let us examine this passage more closely to see whether it is possible on premillennial principles to refer the time about which Jesus was speaking to any other period than the time following the "first resurrection." In the first place, could Jesus be speaking about heaven? Clearly not. The whole point in dispute between the Pharisees and the Sadducees was whether there was or was not a bodily resurrection from the dead. To refer the "out-resurrection" to heaven itself would not only introduce an idea entirely foreign to the discussion of that time between the Sadducees and Jesus, but would violate the fundamental claim of the premillennialists that "ek nekron" refers to the period following the bodily resurrection of the righteous. This term *never,* according to the premillennialists, refers to the period *before* the rapture of believers (except of course the various resurrections in the time of Christ's earthly ministry).

But according to premillennial principles, can it possibly refer to the eternal state *after* the Great White Throne judgment? Of course that *is* the period to which the amillennialists believe it does refer, but according to premillennial principles that would be impossible unless the premillennial principles be abandoned. The premillennialist insists that the righteous are raised a thousand years *before* the resurrection of the wicked, and the term "resurrection from the dead", here used by Jesus, *must* refer to the resurrection of the righteous, because the underlying assumption of both the Sadducees and Jesus was that the woman and her seven husbands were Jews, and that they were righteous, so that they *"attained* to that age and the resurrection from the dead." Had they been unrighteous, Jesus would not have said that those who attained to that age are like the "angels in heaven." It must then be admitted by all that those mentioned are at least Jews, and that they are of the class called "the righteous."

But could not the premillennialist say that while that is true, nevertheless Jesus is talking about the eternal state and not about the millennial kingdom? In order to appreciate the reasons why that would be impossible if there *were* a millennial kingdom to be set up in Palestine, we must consider the historical background of that period when Jesus was talking. Remember that the Jews were expecting a literal restoration of the Jewish kingdom in Palestine, with the Messiah sitting on the throne of David. The Pharisees believed that that kingdom would be preceded by the resurrection from the dead, and that it would immediately follow the resurrection. They knew nothing of any 1000 year Messianic reign, for the Book of the Revelation had not been written, and there was no tradition then current of any such limit to the Messianic reign. All the Old Testament prophecies which spoke of the time element of the kingdom spoke of it as an "everlasting kingdom." There was therefore no distinction in their minds between the Messianic kingdom and the eternal kingdom of God. To them the Messianic kingdom *was* the eternal kingdom, but a *literal earthly* kingdom in which the *Jews* reigned with the Messiah over the world. Now the question of the Sadducees about the woman with seven husbands was meant to reduce that whole idea of that kind of a kingdom in which *resurrected* men and women would live on earth, to an absurdity, by showing that one woman could not be the wife of seven resurrected men. The Sadducees were clearly talking about the condition of things *immediately* following the resurrection, though they were trying to prove that the idea of a resurrection involved absurd situations and therefore could not be true. If Jesus did not refer to the same period about which they were talking, He was guilty of deception. There was no possibility that the Divine Son of God could have misunderstood them, so that to say that He began talking about a time 1000 years after the time to which *they* referred without any indication of such a time change, would make Him guilty of subterfuge. No, both Jesus and the Sadducees *must* have referred to the period immediately following the resurrection, and about *that* period Jesus says that there is no marriage, death or sexual life, but that those who take part in that age are like the angels. The amillennialist believes that that state is eternal, and that it follows immediately upon the general resurrection and the final judgment. Every circumstance surrounding the incident in question bears out our contention.

But is there not another possible interpretation of the passage? Might it not be that Jesus is referring to the resurrected Jews of the Old Testament dispensation, and, inferentially, to the people of the church of the New Testament, who are to be changed at the time of the resurrection? In other words might this not refer to the "marriage feast of the Lamb," while there would still be an earthly Jewish kingdom where men died and married and gave birth to children? It would seem that Jesus had foreseen just such a claim, for in His reply to the Sadducees He specifically ruled out such a possible explanation. He declared that they "that are accounted worthy to *attain to that 'age'*, and the resurrection from the dead, neither marry nor are given in marriage." Remember that the Pharisees believed in a Messianic kingdom in which the

Jews *all* took part, particularly those with resurrected bodies. "That age" was the kingdom age, so that attaining to that kingdom age meant of course taking an active part in the kingdom. Now Jesus said that this whole age with *all* its participants was an age in which there was no death or marriage. Whoever enters that age or dispensation will be like the angels. It is hard to see how language could be more definite than the language Jesus used. The whole question at issue was the question of what would be the characteristics of those who took part in the Messianic kingdom following the resurrection, (if there was a resurrection), so that to claim that Jesus was referring to the state of those who were in heaven, or in the air, preceding or during the millennium, and who would be in the resurrected state while there were others who took part in the kingdom on earth with mortal bodies, would again make Jesus guilty of intentional deception or subterfuge.

Whether the period following the resurrection is the eternal kingdom of God or a 1000 year millennium may be open to question, but there can be no question as to the characteristics of those who take part or are present during that age, according to Jesus' own words. They will be like the angels, above mortal passions, and will be immortal. That, however, brings Jesus' own words into direct conflict with the literal interpretation of Old Testament prophecies such as Is. 65:20: "There shall be no more thence an infant of days, nor an old man that hath not filled his days; for the child shall die a hundred years old, and the sinner being a hundred years old shall be accursed." That there should be any such real contradiction is unthinkable for one who believes that the Holy Spirit inspired the Bible. We are shut up to the conclusion, therefore, that the Old Testament prophecies which do so conflict with the New Testament must have other than a literal interpretation.

Now this picture which Jesus gives of the age following the "resurrection from the dead" is the same as that which we find everywhere else in the New Testament. Paul gives the classic description of the state of believers after the resurrection, in I Cor. 15:35-58. This agrees with the picture given in I Thes. 4:13-18. There is no reason anywhere in the New Testament for thinking that those who take part in the age to follow the "first" resurrection will have mortal bodies, after the Second Coming of Christ, and of course all premillennialists believe that the church and the Old Testament saints will be raised with such glorified and immortal bodies. Jesus, however, went beyond that and declared that "they that are accounted worthy to attain to that age and the resurrection of the dead" all have immortal bodies. Gentile or Jew, members of the church or members of the "nations", if they attain at all to that age, they will have immortal bodies according to Jesus.

Negatively, too, Jesus taught that those who are not "worthy" will *not* attain to that age or be present in it. In other words, only the redeemed will be present in the age following the "first" resurrection, again agreeing with the other passages of the New Testament which declare that the wicked will be sent into eternal punishment, (Matt. 25:46).

Among other contradictions between the picture presented by a literal interpretation of the Old Testament prophecies, and the picture which the New Testament paints of the period following the "first" resurrection or the alleged millennium, we wish particularly to call attention to the citizens of the future kingdom. According to the literal interpretation of the Old Testament prophecies, the citizens of the kingdom are Jews, with Gentile nations allowed to come up year by year to worship "the King Jehovah of Hosts, and to keep the feast of the tabernacles" (Zech. 14:16). Any of those who really want to worship in the sanctuary, however, will have to be circumcized, both in heart and in the flesh (Ezek. 44:9). But when we examine the New Testament picture, however, we find that instead of Jews as Jews being the citizens of the kingdom (if there is an earthly millennial kingdom), the citizens who reign with Christ are "the souls of those that had been beheaded for the testimony of Jesus, and the Word of God, and such as worshipped not the beast, neither his image, and received not the mark upon their forehead and upon their hand " (Rev. 20:4). The ones indicated are martyr Christians certainly, and all others who have not worshipped the beast or his image. The word "saint" in the New Testament is always used with reference to Christians, both Jews and Gentiles, so when we find that the camp of the saints is compassed about by the hosts of Satan, in Rev. 20:9, we can only conclude that this refers to Christians, so that it is perfectly plain that the citizenship in the future age following the resurrection of the righteous is to be on a basis of belief in Christ, not on the basis of racial Jewish ancestry or circumcision. Paul says that in Christ, "there is neither Jew nor Greek" (Gal. 3:28), and, "For he is not a Jew who is one outwardly . . . but he is a Jew who is one inwardly; and circumcision is that of the heart, in the spirit, not in the letter" (Rom. 2:28-29). "Beware of the concision: for we are the circumcision, who worship by the Spirit of God, and glory in Christ Jesus, and have no confidence in the flesh" (Philip. 3:3). The "we" referred to Paul and the Philippian Christians, including the Gentile Philippian jailor. These and other passages make it perfectly plain that, as Paul says in Eph. 2:11-22, Gentiles and Christian Jews are both one in Christ Jesus, and that whatever our future destiny may be, there is to be no distinction between Christian Jews and Christian Gentiles.

Nor can it be replied that while that is the condition in the church at present, it will not be the condition in the alleged "millennium." In Rom. 11:14-32 Paul makes it perfectly plain that the only possible way the Jews can get back into the covenant relationship to God is through belief in Christ as Saviour, and being grafted back again into the true olive tree, the kingdom of God of all ages: "And they also if they continue not in their unbelief, shall be grafted in" (verse 23), "and so all Israel shall be saved" (verse 26). Notice that it is the *salvation* of the Jewish race, not its restoration to national prosperity under the Messianic King that is here promised. The context makes it perfectly plain that the only way of salvation is through believing in Christ as Saviour (verse 23), and that salvation is to take place in a racial way for all Jews who are then living, when the total number of the elect Gentiles is complete, at the close of this dispensation. Thus we see that when Jews become Christians, their racial identity is merged into the Christian stream, and the distinction between Jews and Gentiles disappears. They are all one in Christ Jesus, both are in the same "olive tree" (Rom. 11), having the same standing and privileges before God. Not only is there no New Testament warrant for thinking that blessings are promised to the Jews racially, apart from the blessings that come equally to Jews and Gentiles who believe: the contrary would be unthinkable and would violate the teaching that all the blessings we receive in salvation come to us through Jesus Christ and His redemption. If blessings came on any other basis, such as by race, it would indeed be "another gospel" (Gal. 1:8).

So far, we have been pointing out the difficulties and contradictions into which we are plunged if we accept the literal interpretations of all the Old Testament prophecies as the proper method of interpretation. But if we reject the literal method of interpretation as the universal rule for the interpretation of all prophecies, how are we to interpret them? Well, of course, there are many passages in prophecy that were meant to be taken literally. In fact a good working rule to follow is that the literal interpretation of the prophecy is to be accepted unless (a) the passages contain obviously figurative language, or (b) unless the New Testament gives authority for interpreting them in other than a literal sense, or (c) unless a literal interpretation would produce a contradiction with truths, principles or factual statements contained in nonsymbolic books of the New Testament. Another obvious rule to be followed is that the clearest New Testament passages in nonsymbolic books are to be the norm for the interpretation of prophecy, rather than obscure or partial revelations contained in the Old Testament. In other words we should accept the clear and plain parts of Scripture as a basis for getting the true meaning of the more difficult parts of Scripture.

Common sense teaches us that mountains do not have voices with which to break forth into singing, and that trees do not have hands to clap! Such statements are obviously figurative. When a literal interpretation of prophecies such as the temple sacrifices in Ezekiel brings us, as we have shown, into direct conflict with such a doctrine as the all-sufficiency of Christ's sacrifice, then clearly we are justified in searching for a symbolic interpretation of the prophecy. The obvious typology of the tabernacle in the wilderness, leads us naturally to assume that there is a similar interpretation for the temple pictures in Ezekiel. In some cases the symbolism is more clearly evident than in others, but when the literal interpretation plunges us into irreconcilable contradiction with the New Testament, then it is time to look prayerfully for a symbolic interpretation of the prophecies in question.

But the greatest help in the interpretation of prophecies is in the instances in which the New Testament declares prophecies to have been fulfilled in other than a literal way, by some event in the life of Christ or in Apostolic history. One of the most important of such instances is in Peter's Pentecostal address. Peter said of the events of Pentecost, "this is that which hath been spoken through the prophet Joel," and then he quotes from Joel 2:28ff including the passage about the sun being turned into darkness and the moon into blood, and said that this whole passage was fulfilled by the events of Pentecost. Now while there was darkness on the day of Christ's crucifixion, so that the sun might be said to have been turned into darkness, the moon was not literally turned into blood either then or at the time of Pentecost, yet that was a part of the prophecy that Peter said was then fulfilled. If Peter could declare a prophecy like that to be fulfilled when it was obviously not literally fulfilled, then there is certainly great latitude allowed to us in our interpretation of prophecies in the Old Testament. Of course we do not deny that there is still a possibility that such prophecies *may* be more literally fulfilled in the future, but in view of Peter's statement, there is at least the *possibility* that Pentecost was *all* the fulfillment to be looked for in regard to that particular prophecy. Obviously there are *some* at least of the prophecies which can be fulfilled in other than a literal way!

In Acts 15:14-18 James stated that Peter's account of the sending of the Holy Spirit upon the Gentiles agreed with what the prophets had foretold: "I will build again the tabernacle of David, which is fallen, etc." (Amos 9:11-12). Here is a clear instance of prophecy that cannot by any stretch of the imagination be declared to have been literally fulfilled at that time, but James nevertheless quotes it in that connection. Premillennialists are in the habit of insisting that when Gabriel told Mary that God would give to Jesus the "throne of His father David" (Luke 1:32), this must be literally fulfilled in the future in the millennial kingdom, but Peter at Pentecost connected the sitting on that throne with the resurrection of Christ, so that there is the possibility, at least, that Peter regarded the resurrection and ascension of Christ as fulfilling that Davidic prophecy, in the exaltation of Christ as Messianic ruler, (Acts 2:31-36).

But one of the clearest instances in the New Testament of changing the literal meaning of prophecies is in regard to the "children of Abraham" prophecies. The premillennialists are constantly insisting that because so much is made of the promises of Israel in the Old Testament, and because these prophecies have not been literally fulfilled for the people of Israel in the past, there must be a future literal fulfillment in the millennium. Now we would not deny the possibility that God could fulfil these promises that way if He wanted to, but in view of the following facts we do insist that it is not at all *necessary* that we should look for such a literal fulfillment. Paul repeatedly declares that Christians are the *true* Israel. "They that are of the faith, the same are the sons of Abraham" (Gal. 3:7). "If ye are Christ's, then are ye Abraham's seed, heirs according to the promise" (Gal. 3:29). "That he might be the father of them that believe, though they be in uncircumcision" (Rom. 4:11). "For if they that are of the law are heirs, faith is made void, and the promise is of none effect" (Rom. 4:14). "For this cause it is of faith, that it may be according to grace; to the end that the promise may be sure to all the seed; not to that only which is of the law, but to that also which is of the faith of Abraham, who is the father of us all" (Rom. 4:16). "For they are not all Israel that are of Israel: neither because they are Abraham's seed are they all children: but in Isaac shall thy seed be called. That is, it is not the children of the flesh that are the children of God; but the children of the promise are reckoned for a seed" (Rom. 9:7-8). "That the Gentiles should be fellow heirs, and of the same body, and partakers of his promise in Christ by the gospel" (Eph. 3:6). "Wherefore, receiving a kingdom which cannot be shaken, let us have grace" (Heb. 12:28). "Now to Abraham were the promises spoken, and to His seed. He saith not And to seeds, as to many; but as of one, And to thy seed which is Christ" (Gal. 3:16). Now since we are joint-heirs with Christ, (Rom. 8:17), it follows that we are, as Christians, heirs of the promises to Abraham. Moreover, as Christians, "all things are yours" (I Cor. 3:21), including the "things to come" (I Cor. 3:22). We are "heirs of the kingdom which he promised to them that love him" (James 2:5), and this is for all who believe in Christ. From all these passages it is plain that the New Testament teaches definitely that Christians as Christians are the heirs to the promises made to Israel in the past. Whatever the future may hold for the true Israel who are the true heirs to the promises given in the Old Testament, that true Israel will be composed of Christians who are both Jews and Gentiles, who share equally and on the same basis in all those future blessings. We may differ as to when those blessings will come, but that they come to Christian Jews and Gentiles alike solely on the ground of their faith in Christ ought to be a self-evident principle to every Christian who has studied his New Testament.

We have a similar example in the use of the word Zion. All through the prophecies of the Old Testament we have promises to Zion and about Zion, and concerning the restoration of Zion. Typical of these numerous prophecies is the one in Micah 4:7, "And I will make that which was lame a remnant, and that which was cast far off, a strong nation: and Jehovah will reign over them in Mount Zion from henceforth even forever." A literal interpretation of this prophecy would certainly be that Jehovah will establish an earthly kingdom on the literal Mount Zion in Palestine and reign over the restored remnant of the Jews forever. In passing we would call attention to two facts that are rather disconcerting to the theory of a thousand year reign of Christ in Jerusalem. In the first place it is Jehovah who will reign, and it is very doubtful whether the word "Jehovah" is used in the Old Testament exclusively with reference to the Second Person of the Trinity. And second, that the reign is not merely for a thousand years, but is said to be forever. In the New Testament, however, we find Mount Zion used symbolically to denote the invisible kingdom of God, with its seat of government in Heaven. "But ye are come unto Mount Zion, and unto the city of the living God, the heavenly Jerusalem, and to the innumerable hosts of angels, to the general assembly and the church of the firstborn who are enrolled in heaven, and to God, the Judge of all, and to the spirits of just men made perfect, and to Jesus, the mediator of a new covenant, and to the blood of sprinkling that speaketh better than that of Abel" (Heb. 12:22-24). Similarly in I Pet. 2:3-6. "If ye have tasted that the Lord is gracious, unto whom coming, a living stone, rejected indeed of men, but with God elect, precious, ye also, as living stones, are built up a spiritual house, to be a holy priesthood, to offer up spiritual sacrifices, acceptable to God through Jesus Christ. Because it is contained in Scripture, Behold I lay in Zion a chief cornerstone, elect, precious: and he that believeth on him shall not be put to shame." It is quite clear from this that Jesus was the "living stone," the "chief corner stone" in "Zion," while all true Christians are also living stones built up into the spiritual Zion. Notice that the whole temple ritual is said to be fulfilled by Christians: they are priests, constitute the temple, and offer up sacrifices acceptable to God. Is it not plain from this that there is no necessity to interpret any of the prophecies about the restored temple, the priesthood, sacrifices or Zion itself, literally? They are all symbols of the redeemed church of God, the kingdom of God in the spiritual sense, and so fulfil all the prophecies concerning these things in the Old Testament. Of course we cannot prove that the literal fulfillment of such promises is *impossible* in the future, but these New Testament passages indicate that there is no *necessity* for such literal fulfillment, and any literal fulfillment would be completely possible in the eternal kingdom of God to be established after the Great White Throne judgment, if God plans a literal fulfillment, which is to be deemed highly improbable.

But what shall we say about the prophecies concerning the unbelieving Jews? Are they too, symbolical, or are we to expect a literal fulfillment? Well, in the first place there is no evidence that there is any racial prosperity or national restoration promised to the Jews as a people, apart from their acceptance of Christ as Saviour. It is said: "If the number of the children of Israel be as the sand of the sea, it is the remnant that shall be saved" (Rom. 9:27; Is. 10:22). It is salvation, not national restoration that is the great hope of the Jew, and after he is saved, he is on exactly the same basis as the Christian Gentile, as we have shown above. However, for the unbelieving Jew, there are prophecies which we have every reason to expect will be literally fulfilled. Those promises are of wrath and judgment, of being scattered among the nations of the world, and of persecution and tribulation. There is no hint or indication anywhere in the New Testament that such prophecies are to be interpreted in any other way than literally. In fact the persistence of the Jewish race in the world and the constant persecution to which they have been subjected, is one of the wonders of prophecy fulfilled before our eyes. Nothing but wrath and destruction awaits the race unless they turn to Christ and accept him as their Saviour and Messiah. Then they will be restored to their rightful part in the true church of God in which there is neither Jew nor Gentile, and share in the blessings promised to the spiritual children of Abraham.

In conclusion, then, we sum up the whole situation in regard to the fulfillment of the eschatological promises in the Old Testament by pointing out that we are to look for a literal fulfillment of these prophecies except when such literal fulfillment conflicts with truths, doctrines or principles taught in the New Testament, and unless there is plain authority in the New Testament for taking the items of the prophecy in other than a literal sense. In general we are to follow the example of the New Testament and interpret items of prophecy symbolically when the New Testament so interprets them.

NOTE. In this chapter it is not intended to claim that *all* premillennialists hold that bloody sacrifices will be reinstituted in the alleged millennial temple. They appreciate too well that such sacrifices would conflict with the "once-for-all" character of Christ's sacrifice on the cross. We point out here, however, that if the principle of literal interpretation of the Old Testament prophecies is followed, there is no more reason for discarding the temple sacrifices than for discarding other parts of the prophecies which are not figurative in form. If it be admitted that the temple sacrifices should be discarded because they are inconsistent with the teachings of the New Testament, then the whole principle of literal interpretation of prophecies has been discarded, and other parts can be discarded for similar reasons, and interpreted symbolically.

Chapter VI

THE PARABLE OF THE WHEAT AND THE TARES

24 "THE kingdom of heaven is likened unto a man that sowed good seed in his field; 25 but while men slept, his enemy came and sowed tares also among the wheat, and went away. 26 But when the blade sprang up and brought forth fruit, then appeared the tares also. 27 And the servants of the householder came and said unto him, Sir, didst thou not sow good seed in thy field? Whence then hath it tares? 28 And he said unto them, An enemy hath done this. And the servants say unto him, Wilt thou then that we go and gather them up? 29 But he saith, Nay, lest haply while ye gather up the tares, ye root up the wheat with them. 30 Let both grow together until the harvest: and in the time of harvest, I will say to the reapers, Gather up first the tares, and bring them in bundles to burn them; but gather the wheat into my barn. . . 37 He that soweth the good seed is the Son of man; 38 the field is the world; and the good seed these are the sons of the kingdom; and the tares are the sons of the evil one; 39 and the enemy that sowed them is the devil; and the harvest is the end of the age; and the reapers are angels. 40 As therefore the tares are gathered up and burned with fire; so shall it be in the end of the age. 41 The Son of man shall send forth his angels, and they shall gather out of his kingdom all things that cause stumbling, and them that do iniquity, 42 and shall cast them into the furnace of fire: there shall be weeping and gnashing of teeth. 43 Then shall the righteous shine forth as the sun in the kingdom of their father." (Matt. 13:24-30, 36-43).

It is a well-known rule of exegesis to proceed from the plain and explicit to the obscure and ambiguous. In dealing with such a disputed subject as eschatology, it is well to follow the same rule, instead of starting with a passage that is in the midst of a figurative and symbolical book, about which there is legitimate difference of opinion as to the correct interpretation. Therefore instead of beginning with the 20th chapter of Revelation, as do the premillennialists, is it not well to begin with a passage about whose meaning there can be no room for legitimate differences of opinion? Certainly in all of Scripture there would seem to be no passage plainer than the passage quoted above, the parable of the wheat and the tares, and the interpretation of the parable by Christ Himself. All the facts of eschatology are not given in this parable, but what *has* been given is authoritative. Other additional items in the eschatological picture may be given later, but there can be no legitimate difference of opinion about the meaning of the points here revealed by Christ, for He has explained them Himself. If any interpretation of other passages in the New Testament conflicts with what is here plainly revealed, then such an interpretation must be branded as false. It is unthinkable that the omniscient Son of God, even in His state of humiliation, should have claimed to have knowledge which He did not have, or that He should have, either intentionally or unintentionally, made statements calculated to lead men astray. Later revelations to others may and do *add* to the knowledge of last things revealed to us, but they cannot and will not *contradict* what is plainly revealed in this parable. Because the Lord Himself interpreted the parable to us in plain unequivocal words, the parable gives us the norm for the interpretation of last things. We are bound by that interpretation, and have no right to ignore or to minimize the truth here revealed.

In the kingdom parables of the 13th chapter of Matthew, Christ is illustrating various aspects of the kingdom of heaven. In this parable, whatever may be said of the others, clearly the kingdom of heaven here mentioned is manifested in this world, in this present age. Placing the time in the future, after the Second Coming of Christ, would violate the plain sense of the whole parable. The central truth of the parable is that the sons of the kingdom and the sons of the evil one, live together in the world until judgment day. It is the truth that the Psalmist put so clearly in the words, "Fret not thyself because of evil doers. . . . for they shall soon be cut down like the grass " (Ps. 37:1-2). The Christian is not to be discouraged at the seeming prosperity of the wicked, for it is the plan of God to allow them to exist in the world until the day of judgment, when they will be cast into the furnace of fire. The present age, then, is to be an age of mixture of good and evil. That mixture does not mean that the King does not have the *power* to eliminate the evil now, but that He has chosen to postpone the day of reckoning until the time of the harvest.

Now this is the principal teaching of the parable given so plainly that no one has a right to question its meaning. But while giving this central lesson, Christ also gave us a great amount of information about the events of the last days. Notice first that the *kingdom of heaven* is like the illustration of the parable, or rather that the kingdom of heaven *is* the condition of things described in Christ's interpretation of the *meaning* of the parable. Jesus tells us what the parable teaches, so we know that the kingdom of heaven is that which He describes, namely the whole body of believers in the world itself, associated with the children of the devil. In other words, the kingdom of heaven is the condition of things in this present age here on earth, and the Son of Man is the king, now, of His kingdom. He will continue as king up to the time of the judgment, at the end of the age. If there is to be a millennium on earth in the future, it does not appear in this parable. In the last verse, "then shall the righteous shine forth as the sun in the kingdom of their Father " (Matt. 13:43), it would seem to be taught that the eternal Kingdom of God immediately succeeds the judgment referred to, with no 1000 year intermission.

Then next, notice the field is the *world,* not the church. There is no justification for the view that this parable teaches that there should be no discipline in the church. The visible church as such is not mentioned in the parable, while what appears is the invisible church in the whole world. Similarly, the sons of the evil one are not merely the unbelievers inside the visible church, but all the unbelievers in the whole world who are the children of the devil. Their true nature may not appear until they bring forth fruit, but they are tares from the beginning until the end, just as the wheat is wheat and nothing else from the planting of the seed to the time of the harvest. These two classes of people may resemble each other for a time, and they may be closely associated, but no one from one class ever gets into the other. This whole parable certainly disproves the claims of the postmillennialists, for it is clearly taught that both classes of people will be in the world right up to the judgment day.

Now notice next that the *harvest* is at the end of this age. Some premillennialists insist that the end of the age may stretch over a thousand years, but the word here used, "sunteleia," really means "consummation," and is used only six times in the New Testament, while the verb from which it is taken, "sunteleo," is used 7 times in the New Testament and always has the meaning of "completing" or "finishing" or "ending" things. There is no warrant from the use of these words in the New Testament for thinking that this "end" can be stretched over a 1000 year period. The only length of time is just that required for the harvest, that is, the judgment itself, which finishes this age. The introduction of a new age, the millennial age, after the present age is simply outside this picture. Another age could not by any fair treatment be called the end of this present age. At the time of the harvest, that is, the judgment, the wicked are sent to eternal punishment in the furnace of fire.

Then notice next that the wicked are gathered *out of the kingdom* of the Son of Man. In other words, the kingdom of the Son of Man *precedes* the harvest, and the harvest is at the close of this present age. There is no indication in the passage that there is another later kingdom called the millennial kingdom on earth as distinct from the eternal kingdom mentioned in verse 43. This whole picture agrees with the turning over of his kingdom by Christ to the Father, mentioned in I Cor. 15:24.

The next point to notice is that *all* evil men are gathered out of the kingdom of the Son of Man. If all are gathered, there will be none left. The premillennialist claims that there will be evil men left on earth in the generic group called "the nations," during the millennium, and that Christ will rule over them with a rod of iron. But it is said in this parable that all are gathered *out of* the kingdom, and sent into the furnace of fire, so there would be none left to rule over during the millennium if there is one to follow this time. Since also, as we have shown in Chapter V, Christ said that there will be no marriages in the next age, and since according to premillennialists the wicked dead are not raised until after the 1000 years, there would be no wicked for Satan to gather "as the sands of the sea" to make war upon the saints, in Rev. 20:8-9. This proves that the premillennial interpretation of Rev. 20 must be wrong, and that the war there mentioned must, as the amillennialist claims, be at the close of this present age before Christ's Second Coming. The fire which comes down from heaven to destroy them, Rev. 20:9, is the same as the fire in the picture described in II Thes. 1:7-10, "at the revelation of the Lord Jesus from heaven with the angels of His power in flaming fire, rendering vengeance to them that know not God, and to them that obey not the Gospel of our Lord Jesus; who shall suffer punishment, even eternal destruction from the face of the Lord and from the glory of His might, when he shall come to be glorified in His saints."

Now it is true that in this parable nothing is said of either the righteous or the wicked dead. However, since the picture is of the whole interadventual period, does not the story seem to imply that those who die in the period are included in the fate of the wheat in the parable of the wheat and the tares? Now all admit that the righteous dead are raised at the same time the living righteous are glorified, so that they too "shine forth as the sun in the kingdom of the Father " (Matt. 13:43), and since the tares are said to be gathered *first,* is it not logical to infer that the wicked dead are also among those raised and "gathered into bundles to burn them"? (Matt. 13:30). The mere fact that the wicked dead are not specifically mentioned cannot be used as an argument against their being raised and sharing in the judgment picture, since the righteous dead are also not mentioned, and premillennialists agree that they are raised at this time. The fact remains that it is implied that all the wheat and all the tares are associated together throughout the interadventual period, and that would imply that they both share in the judgment at the end of this age.

But according to this parable just where would the premillennialist insert the millennium? The whole context implies that the parable deals with the present age, so it could not be claimed that it describes the millennium. Were it the millennium the "wheat" would have been raptured at the beginning of the period and not be living along side of the "tares" as they are in the parable. Moreover the fact that Christ says that the field *is* the world, implies that it is the present age that he is talking about. But if it is not the present age, then the millennium must be inserted *after* the events here described. The only place where it could possibly be inserted is between verses 41 and 42, or between 42 and 43. If it is inserted between verses 41 and 42, then we have the spectacle of the millennial kingdom being placed *after* the kingdom of the Son of Man! The assumption of the premillennialist is that the kingdom of the Messiah follows His Second Coming, while this would make two kingdoms for the Son of Man, one preceding the Second Coming and one following the other. The same would hold true if the millennium be inserted between verses 42 and 43, with the added argument that the wicked will have already been sent to the furnace of fire, so that there would be none left on earth for

Satan to gather at the close of the millennium. Certainly no one reading the parable with an open mind would get any other teaching than that the present age is the kingdom of the Son of Man, that the true believers and the children of the devil live together till the end of the age, that the judgment then occurs, that the wicked are then sent to eternal punishment and that the eternal kingdom of God follows immediately as the next eschatological event.

Chapter VII

THE SECOND COMING ACCORDING TO CHRIST

IN the 24th chapter of Matthew, and the parallel passages in Mark 13:1-37, and Luke 21:5-36, we have the account of the Second Coming of Christ in His own words. The passages are too long to quote, but the first thing to notice about them is that they are called forth by a three-fold question asked him by the disciples: (1) When will the foretold destruction of Jerusalem take place? (2) What will be the sign of Jesus' Second Coming? (3) What is the sign of the end of the world? (Matt. 24:3). In the Mark and Luke passages the questions are all put into one two-headed question as to the time and the sign when Jesus' prophesied destruction of the temple was to take place. While a good deal in the Luke passage is similar to that in Matthew, it seems evident from Luke 21:21 and 21:24 that Luke regarded the whole discourse as referring principally to the destruction of Jerusalem, though the phrase, "but the end is not immediately," in Lk. 21:9, is open to the interpretation that it refers to the end of the age, while in 21:8, apparently Jesus is referring to His own Second Coming: "Take heed that ye be not led astray: for many shall come in my name, saying, I am he." This however might refer to the period before the destruction of Jerusalem and probably does so refer, for all that Jesus says is that He is *not* coming at that time. But in Lk. 21:25-28, the Second Coming is definitely referred to.

In the Mark passage it is more difficult to determine whether the words are to be confined to the events connected with the destruction of Jerusalem or whether they refer also to the tribulation preceding the Second Coming, since the words are almost the same as those in Matthew. In Mark 13:21-27 apparently the principal reference is to the Second Coming.

In the Matthew passage which contains the three questions quoted above, the answer Jesus gives is apparently a general one to all three questions without distinction or with very little distinction between the questions. It is as though He were looking into the future with all the events painted on a great screen, with no perspective in time, while He describes simply what He sees in the whole picture. It seems probable that the tribulation described is not merely the tribulation at the time of the destruction of Jerusalem, but the great tribulation preceding the coming of Christ. Similarly the wars and earthquakes seem to be the ones in the end time. There is no question but that from Matt. 24:13-14 He is talking about the end of the age, but in the following verses, 15-22, the principal reference seems to be to the events preceding the destruction of Jerusalem, though the final tribulation may also be in view, of which the Jerusalem destruction was a type. From verse 23 onward the reference is clearly to the Second Coming, the Great Tribulation preceding it, and the end of the age.

Now from the whole description we discover the following facts: (1) At the end of the age there will be wars and earthquakes Matt. 24:6-8, (2) False christs and false prophets will arise, Matt. 24:24, (3) If the abomination of desolation refers to the Anti-christ, then he arises about that time, Matt. 24:15, (4) The great tribulation occurs at this time, Matt. 24:21, 29, (5) *After* the great tribulation signs in the heavens appear, Matt. 24:29, (6) The Son of Man then comes on the clouds with power and great glory, Matt. 24:30, (7) At the coming of Christ a separation between men will occur, some taken and others left, apparently referring to the rapture, Matt. 24:40-41, (8) We are warned to be ready at any time for Christ will come when we do not expect him, Matt. 24:42-51, (9) Apparently the judgment day is referred to in Matt. 24:51.

From all this it is clearly apparent that the same order of events as in the parable of the wheat and the tares is in view, with the addition of some new items to the eschatological picture. Apparently the good and the evil are both to be present when Christ comes (Matt. 24:30, 39-41, 51). The judgment apparently follows immediately (Matt. 24:51). The new items in the picture are the wars and earthquakes, the false prophets and christs, the abomination of desolation, and the great tribulation. The most important point for our discussion is the fact that the great tribulation, Matt. 24:29, unquestionably precedes Christ's coming in the clouds with power and great glory, at which time (not seven years previously) there is the sound of the great trumpet and the elect are gathered from one end of heaven to the other, referring either to the resurrection or to the gathering of the souls of the dead saints. Very clearly there is no reference to a *secret* rapture in the words, "one is taken and the other left," for the comparison is between the days of Noah and the Second Coming, while the mention of the Second Coming is to the coming on the clouds (Matt. 24:30, 36-40). Apparently the judgment occurs at the time referred to when Christ comes, for the tribes of the earth mourn and there is weeping and gnashing of teeth (Matt. 24:30, 51).

There is no mention of any millennium or reign of Christ to follow the events mentioned in this chapter. Of course this argument from silence is inconclusive, but the fact remains that if there is a millennium, Christ has not mentioned it here. As we will see in the following chapter, the judgment occurs at the time when Christ comes in glory (Matt. 25:31).

Chapter VIII

THE JUDGMENT OF THE SHEEP AND THE GOATS

IN Matthew 25:31-46 we have a judgment picture which is commonly called the "sheep and goat judgment." The similar features of this judgment, the judgment mentioned in II Thes. 1:7-10, the judgment scene in the parable of the wheat and the tares and the judgment scene in Rev. 20:11-15 commonly called the Great White Throne judgment, would seem to indicate that all these judgments are at the same time, when Christ comes in the clouds with power and great glory, and that the living and the dead are punished in one great judgment scene. That is the natural interpretation of the various passages and the obvious one. In fact even some premillennialists identify the sheep and goat judgment with the Great White Throne judgment (e.g. Wm. B. Riley, "The Evolution of the Kingdom," p. 139ff). However, most premillennialists realize that to identify all these judgments with one great judgment scene involves their premillennial theory with hopeless difficulties, for in the parable of the wheat and the tares, the tares are gathered into bundles to burn them, *before* the wheat is gathered into the barns, while both grow together in this present age, until the end of the age, when the harvest comes. If that is done, then there will be no room for the millennium with the "wheat" raptured at least 1000 years before the tares are judged, for the Lord specifically says that the angels are to let both grow together till the harvest, and then the reapers, the angels, are to gather up *first* the tares, and *then* they are to be burned with fire. Similarly in the II Thes. 1:7-10 passage, if the time when the judgment takes place is "when He shall come to be glorified in His saints and to be marvelled at in all that believed," in other words, at the time of the Great White Throne judgment, there would again be no room for the millennium. Similarly, in the case of the sheep and goat judgment, it is said that "when the Son of Man shall come in His glory, and before Him shall be gathered all the nations; and He shall separate them one from another....Then shall he say to them on the left hand, Depart from me ye cursed into eternal fire which is prepared for the devil and His angels, and these shall go away into eternal punishment, but the righteous into eternal life" (Matt. 25:31-46). This clearly defines the time of the judgment and the punishment as the time when the Son of Man comes in glory, so that if it coincides with the Great White Throne Judgment, there would be no room for the millennium.

These difficulties are realized by most premillennialists, so they seek to escape the force of them by placing the other judgments at the beginning of the millennium and the Great White Throne judgment at the close of the millennium. It is now our purpose to show that such a position involves the premillennial position in still greater difficulties.

It is a cardinal principle of premillennialism that there must be unbelieving nations present on the earth during the alleged millennium, ruled over by Christ with a rod of iron, because at the close of the millennium Satan is said to be loosed for a time to deceive the nations and to gather them to war against the saints (Rev. 20:7-9). It is asserted that every knee is forced to bow to the Messiah King during the millennium, but that these nations are still rebellious at heart.

Now when we consider the sheep and goat judgment we learn some interesting things. In the first place, according to premillennial assumptions, the wicked dead do not rise until the end of the millennium, so of course they will not be present on the earth during the alleged millennium. However, notice that the living wicked according to Matt. 25:31 must be included in the nations who are gathered before the judgment throne of Christ for it says that *all* the nations are gathered before the Son of Man and judged. Now when it says *all* the nations I believe we must interpret it literally as *all* without exception. Not one single living member of the group called "the nations," whoever they may be, will be left out. They will all be gathered and judged. Now notice their destiny. "Then shall he say unto them on the left hand, Depart from me, ye cursed, into the eternal fire which is prepared for the devil and his angels. . . .And these shall go away into eternal punishment: but the righteous into eternal life" (Matt. 25:41,46). Could anything be plainer? All the living members at least of the "nations," will be judged, and the "goats" will be sent into "the eternal fire prepared for the devil and his angels." There will therefore be none of this group of "the nations" left to go into the millennium (if there is an earthly millennium).

The force of this whole argument is such that various premillennialists try to escape it in a number of different ways. In the first place some premillennialists claim that when it speaks of the "nations," they are thought of in a national sense, not an individual sense, so that the judgment is one of nations not individuals as such.[22] A close examination of the passage shows at once how ridiculous such a claim is. How could nations as such, in the national sense, take in the "brethren," or visit them in prison? But even were we to say that nations are dealt with in a national sense, that does not solve the premillennialists's problem, for we would have to say that they are sent "into eternal fire," as nations, all nationally condemned to eternal punishment because of their treatment of the "brethren." But if they as nations are sent into eternal fire, how could the individuals in the nations escape the same fate? If the nation as a whole is punished, then the whole includes all parts, the individuals in the nations, so we would be in the same difficulty as before, and would face the fact that there would be no wicked nations or individuals left on earth during the alleged millennium!

Other premillennialists have tried to claim that only representatives of the nations are thus judged and sentenced, while others would be left to go into the millennium. Such reasoning is certainly wresting the plain meaning of the text, for nothing there is said about representatives, and the text distinctly says that "all" the nations are gathered for the judgment, and every indication in the text is that they are all separated into "sheep" and "goats," and that the goats are all sent into eternal fire. If language means anything it is plain that this teaches the absolute separation of *all* the individuals in the nations into two classes, and the condemnation of one whole class into eternal fire. The departure is, to all appearances, immediate upon receipt of the command from Christ to enter into eternal fire. According to any sane interpretation of this passage there would be no wicked left on earth after the sheep and goat judgment.

It will not do for the premillennialists to claim that other passages teach that there will be unbelieving "nations" on the earth during the millennium, (e.g. Zech. 14:16-19, etc.), for even were there no other possible interpretation of such passages (and there is another interpretation of them), it would merely mean that those passages contradicted this plain teaching of Christ about the judgment. No premillennialist who believes that the Bible is the Word of God could believe that the Bible contains real contradictions.

But we find the same teaching in the II Thes. 1:7-10 passage. *All* those who "know not God and who obey not the Gospel of our Lord Jesus," will be punished with eternal destruction from the face of the Lord and from the glory of His might, "when he shall come to be glorified in His saints." This passage clearly teaches that all ignorant heathen and all disobedient Gentiles or Jews who obey not the Gospel, will be punished with eternal punishment at the time of the Second Coming. All these judgment passages clearly teach that all the living wicked at least are punished when the judgment occurs, so that if the time be declared to be at the beginning of an alleged millennium, then at that time there will be no living wicked left to go into the millennium. All, without exception, will go into eternal punishment then.

There are, it is true, many instances in the New Testament in which the word "all" does not mean literally *all* without exception. In many cases it means all of the classes under discussion, or all in a rhetorical sense used of a great number, as, "your faith is proclaimed throughout the whole world" (Rom. 1:8), the word "whole" here having a similar meaning to "all," and meaning simply "widely" where they were mentioned at all. But in the passage we are discussing the class under discussion includes literally *all* nations, who are all gathered for judgment. How would it be possible for any nation to escape the "all" who are thus judged? Could we imagine that some nation would escape from the angels who gather them to judgment? And when dealing with such a subject as judgment, there would be no justice in the judgment if only part of the nations were judged. The very essence of God's judgment is that He judges according to truth and righteousness, and both truth and righteousness demand that in such a judgment scene the judgment shall be complete and thorough, leaving no nation or part of the nation out of the judgment. But if this is done, then there would be literally no single unbelieving wicked man or woman in the whole wide world who would escape the condemnation to eternal fire.

But, as we have shown in Chapter V, in Luke 20:34-36, while talking to the Sadducees about the resurrection, Jesus says that those who attain to the "resurrection from the dead" "neither marry nor are given in marriage, neither can they die any more; for they are equal to the angels." Is it not perfectly plain that since the living wicked were all sent to eternal fire, and the wicked dead, according to the premillennialist, have not yet been raised, while the righteous will all have entered heaven at the time of the rapture, and will not bear children during the millennium, there will be no wicked nations on the earth during the alleged millennium, and therefore none whom Christ could rule over with the rod of iron, so that there would be left no nations for Satan to deceive at the close of the millennium when he is said to gather them in number like the "sands of the sea?" Is it not plain, therefore that there must be another explanation of the Rev. 20:7-9 passage about the deceit of the nations by Satan? The other explanation is of course that that whole passage refers to the time *before* Christ's Second Coming, when the Satan-deceived nations gather at the Battle of Armageddon.

But perhaps it may be replied that the righteous will not be on the earth during the millennium, and therefore the Luke 20:34-36 passage does not refer to conditions on the earth, since only the Jews rule over the nations during the 1000 years under the king-ship of Christ. In reply we call attention to the fact that the people under discussion by both the Sadducees and Jesus were certainly *at least* the Jews, since the Jewish woman and her seven husbands were certainly Jews. If they *attain* to that age, whether it is the millennial age as the premillennialist declares, or the eternal kingdom of God as the amillennialist believes, the Jews will certainly be like the angels according to what Jesus said. Since they are like the angels they will not have children during that alleged millennium!

Thus all the Gentile nations would be judged, at the sheep and goat judgment, and sent either to eternal punishment or eter-nal life; all the Jews who "attain to that age" (or Gentiles either for that matter) will have bodies like those of the angels, so that no wicked nations could be born to either Jews or Gentiles during the alleged millennium, and no wicked nations would be left after the sheep and goat judgment to enter the millennium! There would therefore be no people from any possible source (since the wicked dead have not been raised at that time according to the premillennialist) who would be wicked at heart, for Christ to rule over with a rod of iron, and who would be gathered by Satan at the close of the millennium!

Is it not clear that the premillennial assumptions lead into hopeless contradictions, whether the judgment passages be placed at the beginning or the end of the alleged millennium? The only sane interpretation is the obvious one that all the judgments mentioned are the same judgment, when both the dead and the living are gathered before the great white throne after they have both been raised and raptured or, in the case of the wicked, gathered for judgment before the throne of Christ. After the general resurrection and the rapture of the righteous, the final judgment follows at once, and the eternal kingdom is set up.

Some premillennialists have tried ingeniously to escape the force of this argument by declaring that the sheep and goat judgment does not separate absolutely between the saved and the unsaved, but simply separates on the basis of the way the peoples have treated the Jews, and that those who are declared to be "righteous" in Matt. 25:37, may be only *relatively* righteous, so that they enter into the millennium with unregenerated hearts, or even with regenerated hearts but with mortal bodies capable of giving birth to children. These children would then be gathered at the close of the millennium by Satan!

The difficulty with such a view is that Jesus said, in Luke 20:34-36, that *all* who attain to that age and the resurrection from the dead, have bodies like the angels, so that whether "absolutely" or only "relatively" righteous, before they entered "that age," their bodies would be rendered incapable of bearing children! All unbelievers at the time *when* Christ comes, according to II Thes. 1:7-10, are to suffer eternal destruction from the face of the Lord, so they could never get into the alleged millennium "relatively" righteous, but not absolutely righteous in the sense of being saved. If they get into "that age," the age after the Second Coming, whether it is the millennium or the eternal kingdom of God, it will be with glorified bodies like the angels.

The simple interpretation of the sheep and the goats as leaving no one on earth without glorified bodies after this judgment, and therefore no one would give birth to children during the alleged 1000 years following that judgment so that Satan could gather them as "sands of the sea, at the close of the millennium, seems perfectly obvious to one who examines the passages Luke 20:34-36, and Matt. 25:31-46 with unprejudiced mind. A noted conference leader and missionary who holds to the historic premillennial view makes an ingenious attempt to evade the force of the above argument. He declares that the righteous "sheep" of the Matt. 25:31ff passage are not raptured saints at all, but are another class of Gentiles who were not previously regenerated. They accept Christ at the very instant of His pronouncing them "blessed of my Father," and then have eternal life but are not given glorified bodies. They then enter the millennial kingdom with natural bodies and beget children whose descendants rebel under Satan at the close of the alleged millennium.

There are many difficulties connected with such a view, however. In the first place, even were it true that these "sheep" were not regenerated before the time of the judgment scene (an extremely strange supposition in view of the context), they would nevertheless be regenerated when they believe as they are acquitted before the Throne of Christ. They would certainly then be included in the group who "attain to that age" (Luke 20:35) immediately following the judgment scene. Therefore according to Jesus they would have bodies like the angels in heaven and would be unable to beget children. Since the living wicked are all sent to eternal punishment at that time, they would not be around to beget children during the time of the alleged millennium.

In the second place, it is preposterous to think that any group of Gentiles would be rewarded with eternal life because of their kindness to God's people, while they were in an unregenerated state as this view postulates. Were it true it would be a form of salvation by works, for their kindness to the people of God would be the reason for their being declared "blessed" by Jesus. This would be contrary to all the teachings of Scripture about grace, (cf. Rom. 3:20, 28; Gal. 3:11; Eph. 2:8, 9; Acts 13:39 etc.)

In the third place, were it true that these "sheep" were not regenerated before the time of the rapture, but were regenerated later before the Judgment Throne of Christ, it would be a form of "a second chance," a doctrine which evangelical Christians have all rejected, and which has no Biblical basis whatever.

In the fourth place, in verse 46, "And these shall go away into everlasting punishment but the righteous into eternal life," the only possible interpretation is that the "life eternal" here mentioned is the eternal state of the redeemed, not the eternal life of the believer beginning at the time of regeneration, for they are already declared to be righteous in verse 37, and therefore already justified, so that they are rewarded, not with regeneration, but with the eternal life which is in heaven or in the new heavens and the new earth. They are already regenerated before verse 46, and therefore already have eternal life in the sense of the new birth.

This whole group of "sheep" are clearly the same as those who are raptured at the time of the coming of Christ, and they are saved by grace not by their kindness to the children of God. That kindness is the visible evidence of the condition of their hearts. The judgment of the sheep and the goats simply is the formal public recognition of their saved standing before Christ. Unless the amillennial explanation of Rev. 20:8, 9, namely that it refers to the battle of Armageddon of Rev. 19, is accepted, the problem of where such wicked as numerous as the "sands of the sea" could come from is insoluble for the premillennialist, for only those with spiritual bodies will be around after the judgment of the sheep and goats.

But before leaving this subject we would dwell a little longer on the incongruity of the view that there might be some who were regenerated at the beginning of the alleged millennium, but who would not be given glorified bodies. This view of the "pretribulationists" is that the church is raptured at the beginning of the seven year period, but that through the preaching of the remnant during the seven years, many people on earth believe, and though the great majority are slain and then resurrected at the close of the seven years when Christ comes to earth, a few, at least, escape death and though regenerated, enter the millennium with mortal bodies, giving birth to children who are those whom Satan gathers at the close of the millennium in the great rebellion at that time, when their number is "as the sands of the sea" (Rev. 20:8). As we have pointed out in the preceding paragraph, Christ said that all who "attain to that age" have glorified bodies, and are like the angels, so of course do not give birth to children. That fact alone is sufficient to settle the question for anyone who accepts the Bible as the Word of God. If any one enters the alleged millennium he will have a body incapable of giving birth to children.

But aside from that conclusive fact, notice the incongruity according to the assumption in question, of the great body of the redeemed receiving glorified bodies at the time of the rapture or at the time of the resurrection of the "tribulation saints" at the close of the alleged seven year period, while a few true believers, who would be saved just as truly as the others, would be penalized simply because they were not *killed* during the tribulation! They might have gone through all kinds of tortures, but simply because they escaped death, though they remained faithful to the end, they would be denied (by our pretribulation friends) the blessings of glorification! Could anything be more incongruous? Moreover, according to their assumptions, the Holy Spirit would be removed from the earth during the tribulation period, so how could they have believed in the first place without the quickening power of the Holy Spirit? Though we called them "regenerated" in the preceding paragraph, how could they be regenerated if there were no Holy Spirit present to give them the New Birth? This whole inference deny that man is dead in sin thus contradicting Eph. 2:1, "Ye who were dead in trespasses and sins did He make alive," and since it would teach that man could believe in Christ without the power or presence of the Holy Spirit. But we have pointed out the fact that it would directly contradict the words of Christ when He said that "they that are accounted worthy to attain to that age" are like the angels in heaven, so of course they would not bear children.

Of course, if it be admitted that all true believers are given spiritual bodies at the time of Christ's coming to earth, then they will not beget children, and there will be no one on earth at the close of the millennium (if there be one) whom Satan could deceive at the close of the millenium, since the "goats" were all sent to eternal fire at the beginning of the millennium. This in turn drives us back to the same conclusion that the premillennial interpretation of Rev. 20:7-10 is false, and that that chapter is a picture of events preceding the Second Coming of Christ, instead of what will follow the Second Coming.

Chapter IX

WHO ARE "THE NATIONS" AND WHO ARE THE "BRETHREN"?

THERE is a premillennial claim in connection with the Sheep and Goat Judgment that needs separate discussion. It is claimed that the phrase "the nations," in Matt. 25:32, "And before Him shall be gathered all nations, and he shall separate them one from another, as a shepherd separateth the sheep from the goats," must refer only to the Gentile or non-Jewish nations, and cannot include the Jews, for according to their theory the Jews are "the brethren" of Matt. 25:40, and the Gentiles are to be separated into the sheep and the goats, not on the basis of their acceptance of Christ as Saviour, but only on the basis of how they have treated the Jews, who are "the brethren"![23]

Before dealing with this claim let us point out what we believe to be the true interpretation of the passage. We believe that it is only another facet of the wonderful diamond of salvation. Of course we are saved by grace through faith in Christ, and works even of the kind here mentioned are never the real ground of our acceptance with God as righteous. However, good works *are* the evidence of the *genuineness* of the faith professed, so here they are mentioned as though they were the *actual* ground of acceptance when, in reality, they are only the *evidence* that the actual ground, namely, saving faith, is present in the *hearts* of the "sheep." The acts recorded are *habitual* acts showing the character of the possessor, and indicating what is the true state of the heart of the one who professes belief in Christ. It is only another way of saying, "If ye love me, keep my commandments."

However, the term "ethnos," or "ethne," meaning "nation" or "nations," is a very common term in the New Testament, and it is true that in a majority of cases the contrast is between the Gentiles and the Jews. But this is not always the case. For example, would anyone claim that when Jesus, in the great commission of Matt. 28:19, charged the disciples to "Go ye therefore and teach all nations," he was commanding them *not* to preach to the Jews? In this verse unquestionably the Jews were included in the "all nations." Or would anyone claim that when Paul was addressing the Athenians and said, "God hath made of one blood all nations of men to dwell on all the face of the earth," he is implying that the Jews were of a different "blood" and were not included in the "nations" (Acts 17:26). Or would anyone claim that in Rom. 1:5 Paul does not include the Jews among the "nations" among whom there were those called saints? In fact, there are at least 37 instances in the New Testament in which the phrase "nation" or "nations" refers to the Jewish nation or includes the Jewish nation among the other nations! To insist, therefore, that this phrase in the sheep and goat judgment has a limited meaning when the phrase is made universal, "before him shall be gathered all the nations," and that the Jews are not among those thus judged, has no warrant from Scripture or common sense. No one would ever dream of such an interpretation unless this theory, which is foisted upon Scripture, demanded it.

Equally unjustified from the usage of Scripture, is the claim of the pretribulationist that the word "brethren" in Matt. 25:40, refers to the Jews, and that the basis of the judgment is how well the Gentile nations have treated the Jews! "And the King shall answer and say to unto them, Verily I say unto you, inasmuch as ye have done it unto one of the least of these my brethren, ye have done it unto me." The idea being that those Gentile nations which have given good treatment to the Jews as a race, will enter the millennial kingdom, and those who have mistreated the Jews will be excluded from the millennial kingdom.

Leaving aside the question as to whether it is reasonable to think that the King would call such nations righteous or blessed of His Father, if they were not saved, simply because they had treated non-Christian Jews or even anti-Christian Jews, in a kindly way, we will discuss the question as to the meaning of the "brethren." Before doing so, however, we would point out that there is no Scriptural precedent for calling unsaved people "righteous," nor for calling unsaved people "blessed of my father," so there is every reason for believing that we are dealing only with saved people, the elect believers in Christ as Saviour, who are said to go into eternal life in verse 46 of this chapter. Were any other interpretation accepted, we would have to say that there is another way, through good works, to eternal life, besides the way through belief in Christ as Saviour! But what reason is there for thinking that the "brethren" of Matt. 25:40 are Jewish nationals who are unsaved, or have unsaved among them? There seems to be no reason except that this variety of the premillennial theory demands such an explanation! There is no warrant whatever from the words of Christ, for thinking that He would use the term, in this passage, as applying to unsaved Jews simply because they were of the Jewish race. The word "brethren" is used by Christ himself, referring to "my brethren" or "my brother," only ten times in the Gospels, including this one in Matt. 25:40. These instances are as follows: Matt. 12:48, "Who are my brethren?" Clearly, in conjunction with the following verse in which he says, "Behold my mother and my brethren" (Matt. 12:49), emphasizing that racial or even family ties were not regarded as the closest by Jesus. The same point is emphasized in Matt. 12:50, "Whosoever shall do the will of my Father which is in Heaven, the same is my brother, and sister and mother." The spiritual tie of belief in Christ and obedience to God the Father superceded, with Jesus, the tie of kinship and race, so it is very unlikely that He would make treatment of the Jewish race as such the basis of acceptance with God. In Matt. 28:10, "Be not afraid: go tell my brethren that they go into Galilee, and there shall they see me," again it is the spiritual tie of belief in Christ that is the basis for calling them brethren. The only possible other interpretation of this verse is that He is referring to his kinsmen, the sons of Mary and Joseph. But is it reasonable to think that He was commanding only his brothers, the sons of Mary, to go into Galilee? Certainly the other believers and disciples were included, and even so, the brothers of Jesus were only included because they were believers in His deity and Messiahship. In Mark 3:34; 3:35; and Luke 8:21, we have parallel passages to Matt. 12:48-50. After His resurrection He said, (John 20:17) "Go to my brethren and say unto them, I ascend unto my Father and your Father, to my God and your God," thus clearly calling the disciples "brethren," because of their relationship to their Heavenly Father as sons. It is significant that in every one of these instances, Jesus calls those who do the will of God, that is, true believers in Christ, brethren, and that he never uses the term to include unbelieving Jews! There is no reason whatever for thinking that He used the term any differently in Matt. 25:40, for there He is identifying Himself with the believer, as He did when He told Saul that Saul was persecuting Him when he persecuted the Church.

The term "brethren" is used 12 times in the Gospels by the authors in referring to the brothers and sisters of Christ according to the flesh, who were the children of Mary, His mother, but Christ never refers to them that way Himself. Never does He call the unbelieving Jews, whom he calls "children of your father the devil" (John 8:44), "brethren," and the very thought of applying the term "brethren" to those who killed Him on the cross, is repugnant to one who loves His Lord.

In fact the only cases of its use in the New Testament with reference to unbelievers, are its use by Peter, Stephen and Paul, in public address, when they used the stereotyped form of oratorical address. Except in direct speeches of this kind, the term is never used in the New Testament with reference to unbelieving Jews. The idea that Jesus would so use the term is ridiculous. There is no reason whatever for thinking that He so used the term in Matt. 25:40, where clearly the meaning is that mistreatment of believers is mistreatment of Christ.

Chapter X

THE "ROD OF IRON" RULE BY CHRIST

ONE of the fundamental claims of the premillennialists is that the Messiah will rule over the nations, that is, the Gentile nations, from His millennial capital, Jerusalem, with a stern, just rule, with "a rod of iron," symbolizing forceful, effective rule over people who are rebellious at heart but who are forced to bow to the Messianic rule against their wills.[24] At the close of the alleged millennium Satan is said to gather them to war against the saints (Rev. 20:8), in number as the sands of the sea. This thought of a stern, just rule over rebellious nations during the millennium, is taken from the English translation of three passages in the Revelation, namely, 2:27: "He shall rule them with a rod of iron, as the vessels of the potter are broken to shivers"; 12:5: "And she was delivered of a son, a man child, who is to rule all the nations with a rod of iron: and her child was caught up unto God, and unto His throne"; 19:15: "And out of his mouth proceedeth a sharp sword, that with it he should smite the nations: and he shall rule them with a rod of iron: and he treadeth the winepress of the fierceness of the wrath of God, the Almighty."

At first sight the premillennial argument from these passages for a stern, harsh but just reign of the Messiah over the Gentile nations during the millennium, seems peculiarly strong, particularly the Rev. 12:5 passage. Obviously if these verses are translated correctly, there would be a reasonable presumption that however much other New Testament passages might seem to contradict this thought, we must believe that the Gentile nations will be present during the future Messianic rule, and that they will be forced to obey the stern rule of the Messiah with the "rod of iron." So important is this "rod of iron" rule for the premillennial theory that if the evidence for it breaks down, it would seem to destroy almost the very heart of the premillennial theory.

All three of these passages are obviously quotations from the Septuagint translation of Psalm 2:9, though in place of "rule" the English translations, following the Hebrew text, have "break them with a rod of iron; Thou shalt dash them in pieces like a potter's vessel." The difference between the Hebrew text and the Septuagint translation of this verse, is explained by the fact that Hebrew words for "break" and "rule," have exactly the same consonants but different vowel points. Since the vowel points were added to the Hebrew text about 900 A. D., obviously they are not part of the original inspired text, and represent the interpretation placed on the Hebrew text by the scribes who inserted the vowel points in about 900 A. D. We are at liberty, then, to decide between the two words, "rule" and "break," for the translation of Ps. 2:9. Since Christ and the Apostles used the Septuagint translation as their common text, and since in this place the Apostle John placed his stamp of approval on the use of the word "poimaino" translated "rule" in the English version, there is strong argument for holding that the original Hebrew text intended to use that meaning for the passage in question, Ps. 2:9. We must however notice that the choice of the other meaning, "break them with a rod of iron" would be directly against the premillennial interpretation of the passage, for it would be a prophecy of destruction of the nations, not stern rule. The weight of the evidence nevertheless is in favor of the word "poimaino," translated in the English version, "rule."

The question for discussion, then, is whether the word "rule" correctly translates the Greek word "poimaino." If it is correct, then it would seem to indicate that the Messiah will rule over the

Gentiles with a "stern, harsh, though just rule, in the future millennium" though these nations are said to be rebels at heart and are said actually to rebel under the leadership of Satan at the close of the millennium. It is also interpreted to indicate that there will actually be "the nations," i.e. unsaved Gentile nations, most of whom are forced to bow their knees to Christ, though they are rebels at heart, present during that alleged millennium, in spite of the fact that, as we have shown in the last chapter, all the living wicked are sent to eternal fire at the beginning of the millennium, while all the righteous have glorified bodies so that they could not give birth to children who might become these unsaved "nations." If there is evidence in these verses in Revelation that there is a "rod of iron rule" by Christ in the future, then we will have to accept the rule as a fact in spite of the arguments already given to the contrary.

At first, on the face of it, the argument that "rule" is the correct translation of "poimaino," seems very strong. The various lexicons and versions give this as the meaning, and most of the commentaries also give such a translation for these verses, though Thayer's Lexicon also gives the meaning, "to feed, to tend a flock, to keep sheep," and as a matter of fact in 7 out of the 11 instances of the use of the word "poimaino" in the New Testament, it is actually translated "feed." These instances are Luke 17:7; Jn. 21:16; Acts 20:28; I Cor. 9:7; I Pet. 5:2; Jude 12; and Rev. 7:17. In Matt. 2:6 it is translated "who shall rule my people Israel," but the Revised Version gives "who shall be a shepherd of my people Israel." That would leave only three "rod of iron" passages in Revelation to be translated "rule."

Whenever we want to discover the true meaning of any Greek or Hebrew word, the only safe way is to study the uses of the word in the Bible, and if it is there used too few times, study its use in secular literature of the time. Now in the New Testament there are three words from the same root as "poimaino". These words are "poimnion," "flock," "poimne," "flock," and "poimen," "shepherd." Apparently these words, with the verb "poimaino," are always connected with flocks and shepherds, and the care of flocks. (The word is used once of "feeding cattle," so it was apparently used for feeding any animals or caring for them.) The question immediately arises as to why the word "poimaino" is not translated "feed" or "be a shepherd to" in these remaining passages in Revelation, since it has that meaning universally elsewhere. The answer of course is that there would be no sense to the words "feed them with a rod of iron," so the translators reached the conclusion that "rule" would answer the purpose in the passage. We must notice, however, that in the 39 instances of the use of these four words from the same root, it always elsewhere means "flock," "shepherd," or "caring for the flock" in some way (once in connection with cattle), so the word apparently has a fixed meaning.

Let us now turn to the words "rod of iron" to look for further light on the passages in question. The *Concise Bible Dictionary,* published in connection with the Nelson Bible, says the following in regard to the "rod": "The rod and staff of Ps. 23:4 probably refer to two instruments still used by Eastern shepherds, the first, a heavy-headed club for driving off wild animals, the second a curved stick for guiding the sheep. . . . The shepherd of Palestine carried an oak staff, six feet long, and a weapon, in the form of an oak club, two feet long, (the rod of Ps. 23:4) the thick end of which is studded with nails." *The Students' Commentary* says, p. 314, "He is provided with a club and a crook." Dummelow's *Commentary* says: "The Rod was a short oaken club for defence; the staff a longer pole for use in climbing or leaning upon, and the Eastern shepherd still carries both." In commenting on the Ps. 2:9 passage, Horne says: "Those which continue stubborn and hardened, must be dashed to pieces by the stroke of eternal vengeance."

All this seems to show that the "rod of iron" used in connection with the shepherd word "poimaino," refers not to ruling over the nations with the rod of iron, but to acting toward the nations as a shepherd would act toward wild animals attacking the sheep! How would a shepherd act toward the enemies of the sheep? Certainly by using his rod to dash them to pieces if he could do so! Now for the meaning of the word "poimaino," since it is really equivalent to "being a shepherd," we suggest that a meaning which would exactly fit the root meaning of the word and the context in every place where it is used in the New Testament, is "to act the part of a shepherd." In this case in these "rod of iron" passages, it should be translated, "He shall act the part of a shepherd toward the nations with a rod of iron, as the vessels of the potter are broken to shivers," (Rev. 12:5). That is, the Messiah, to protect His flock, the true people of God, from their enemies, will execute vengeance on the unbelieving nations who have been persecuting God's people. Just as a shepherd would in righteous wrath dash out the brains of the wild beasts who were tearing the lambs to pieces, so the Messiah will vindicate His people with a terrible scene of vengeance upon the enemies of God's people. In other words we have a picture of terrible judgment visited on the wicked nations who have been troubling the Christian saints, the "little flock" of Jesus Christ.

The only justification for translating the word "poimaino" as "rule" in these passages, would be if the nations themselves were the "flock" of the shepherd, Jesus Christ! But no premillennialist would claim that the Gentile nations who are assumed to be in the main rebellious at heart, are the "flock" of the Good Shepherd! The study of these words reveals that the rod is used by the shepherd against enemies, so that unless it were claimed that the unbelieving nations were *protected* from *their* enemies by the Good Shepherd, there would seem to be no possibility of using these words in any other way than that suggested, namely, of the shepherd's dashing them to pieces as a potter's vessel is broken to shivers. The shepherd may, perhaps, be said to "rule over" the flock in a kindly, protecting way, but not with his "rod," and he certainly does not dash his flock to pieces as "a potter's vessel is broken to shivers"! A shepherd's rule over his flock is peaceful and loving, not "stern" and harsh. Imagine a true shepherd striking his sheep with a rod of iron! Sheep have delicate bones, easily broken with a blow of a club! Is it not obvious, even though we did not know that these "rods" are used only to protect the flock from their enemies, that a shepherd would not use his rod of iron *against* his flock? In the new Testament the "flock" of Christ always refers to the elect people of God (e.g., "fear not little flock," Lk. 12:32). The Premillennialist does not believe that the Gentile nations, during the alleged millennium, are the elect people of God, so it would be ridiculous to think of the Messiah king "shepherding" his flock, i. e., the unbelieving Gentile nations, by protecting them from some other enemies, with a rod of iron! If the Gentile nations are the object of the shepherd's activity with the rod of iron, then the only possible activity in view of the context, is that he should *strike* them with the "rod of iron"!

This meaning gives us exactly the same picture as that of II Thes. 1:7-10, when Christ comes, "rendering vengeance to them that know not God, and to them that obey not the gospel of our Lord Jesus; who shall suffer punishment, even eternal destruction from the face of the Lord and from the glory of His might, when he shall come to be glorified in His saints, and to be marvelled at in all them that believed (because our testimony unto you was believed) in that day." The time of the destruction of the nations will be at the time of the sheep and goat judgment of Matt. 25, when the sheep will be separated from the goats, at the time when all the nations are gathered before the judgment throne of the Son of Man and he shall "separate them one from another," and the goats, *all* of them, shall hear His words, "depart from me ye cursed, into the eternal fire which is prepared for the devil and his angels ... and these shall go away into eternal punishment."

Thus we see that the "rod of iron" passages give no justification for thinking that the Messiah will rule over unbelieving nations with a rod of iron during some future kingdom period. These passages all refer to the same picture of vengeance taken by God against the persecutors of God's elect church. The Rev. 19:15 passage, when translated, "And out of His mouth proceedeth a sharp sword, that with it He should smite the nations: and He shall act the part of a shepherd (or, he shall act as a shepherd would act) toward them with a rod of iron; and He treadeth the winepress of the fierceness of the wrath of God, the Almighty," gives us a unified picture of just vengeance against the wicked nations who have followed Satan in war against the saints before the rapture.

So we see that instead of these passages about the "rod of iron" offering a strong argument for premillennialism, they really reinforce our arguments that the wicked are all punished at the same time, when Christ comes again, and that no unbeliever will be left alive on the earth after Christ comes again. They will all be broken to pieces as the "potter's vessel is broken to shivers."

Chapter XI

PAUL'S TEACHING ABOUT THE SECOND COMING

I Corinthians 15:21-26.

"FOR seeing that death came through man, through man comes also the resurrection of the dead. For just as through Adam all die, so also through Christ will all be made alive again. But this will happen to each in the right order—Christ having been the first to rise, and afterwards Christ's people rising at His return. Then cometh the end, when He is to surrender the Kingship to God the Father, when He shall have overthrown all other government and all other authority and power. For He must reign until He shall have put all His enemies under His feet (Ps. 8:6; 110:1). The last enemy that is to be overthrown is Death; for He will have put all things in subjection under His feet" (Translation from the Greek).

In this passage Paul is definitely talking about what is to happen when Christ comes again. The passage on the face of it is a discussion of the resurrection of Christ and the resurrection of the righteous. Nothing is mentioned in the whole passage about the resurrection of the wicked dead; they may be raised at the same time as the other dead, or they may be raised at a different time as far as the evidence here presented is concerned. That subject simply is not discussed by the apostle at all. The wicked dead are not here under discussion, and there was therefore no occasion for the apostle to mention them. No conclusion one way or another is to be drawn as to the time when they are raised, since they are not even mentioned or implied anywhere in the passage. This particular point becomes increasingly important as we examine the teaching of the rest of the passage, for a correct understanding of verse 26 depends upon the fact that only the righteous dead are mentioned or discussed throughout the whole passage.

In this passage Paul apparently teaches that Christ was the first to rise from the dead, but that Christ's people will all rise from the dead when He comes again. At His coming again will be the time of the end of this whole dispensation. It is preceded by the period of time from the first to the second comings of Christ, during which time Christ is the King of His people. But at the end of this dispensation, when the righteous dead are raised, death, the last enemy of Christ, will have been conquered, so that Christ can then turn over the kingdom to the Father, for Christ must reign until He conquers every enemy. Every other enemy will have been conquered when the time of the resurrection of the righteous arrives, and then, with the conquering of death, all His enemies will have been overthrown, and He can turn the kingdom over to the Father.

This seems to be the plain meaning of the passage, and if it is the meaning, certain truths stand out. (1) The period of the kingship of Christ *precedes* the resurrection of the righteous. (2) All other enemies of Christ (including the anti-christ, Satan, and all the hosts of evil) will be overthrown *before* the resurrection of the righteous, for the *last* enemy to be overthrown is death. After the resurrection of the righteous we are not to look for any rebellion under Satan 1000 years later (Rev. 20:8). (3) The resurrection of the righteous is to be followed at once by the turning over of the kingdom of Christ to God the Father.

Now while the above seems to be the plain meaning of this whole passage, the premillennialist declares that it means that Christ's people rise when He returns, then (after a thousand years) comes the resurrection of the remainder of the dead, when He will turn over the Kingdom to God the Father, after overthrowing all other government and power that has been on earth during the millennium. The last enemy, death, will be overthrown at the close of the millennium when there is the resurrection of the wicked.

The crux of this interpretation is in the meaning of two Greek words. The first, "eita," is translated "then," while the second "telos," is translated "end." The premillennialists insist that the first word "eita," in this passage means "later on," so that the passage would read, "Christ having been the first to rise, and afterwards Christ's people rising at His return. Later on cometh the rest (or the remainder)" of the dead. The second word "telos," is thus translated "the rest" or "the remainder."

Let us first examine the evidence in regard to "eita," which our Bibles translate "then." This word is used only ten times in the New Testament, and is not at all the common word for "then." Let us examine the passages in which it is used. (1) "Then cometh the devil and taketh away the word from their heart" (Luke 8:12). This is in the parable of the sower, and refers to the seed sown by the wayside. The seed fell, was trodden under feet, and then the birds devoured it. That is, the people heard the gospel but the devil takes the word away from their hearts before they can believe. Clearly the meaning here is not "later on," but rather "the next event to happen among the events we are considering." (2) "Then he saith to the disciple, Behold thy mother" (John 19:27). While Jesus hung on the cross, after he had said to his mother, "Behold thy son!" next he said to John, "Behold thy mother!" Here clearly there is no long interval of time between the two events. (3) "Peace be unto you. Then saith he to Thomas, Reach hither thy finger and see my hands" (John 20:27). Christ appears after his resurrection, to the disciples, coming through the closed door, utters the salutation and immediately speaks to Thomas. Again there is no long interval of time, but it is the very next event. (4) "Then gifts of healing, helps" (I Cor. 12:28). In this passage no time element is involved, but simply adding another gift of the Spirit to the ones previously mentioned. (5) "Seen of Cephas, then of the twelve" (I Cor. 15:5). Here there is a slight interval of time, but it is the next event among those being discussed. (6) "Seen of James, then of the twelve " (I Cor. 15:7). This is exactly the same as (5). (7) "For Adam was first formed then Eve" (I Tim. 2:13). Here there is a slight interval of time, but it is the next event. (8) "Let these also first be proved; then let them serve as deacons " (I Tim. 3:10). Here the next event in time after the testing of the men, is their appointment as deacons, with no long interval of time involved. (9) "He is drawn away by his own lust, and enticed, then the lust, when it hath conceived, beareth sin" (James 1:15). Here "then" means "next" and clearly involves no long interval of time. (10) The last instance is of course the one under discussion, "Then cometh the end " (I Cor. 15:24). Notice that in none of the other passages is any long interval of time implied. In fact the "later on" translation would hardly fit in any of the passages with the meaning "after a long interval." As a matter of fact there was another Greek word that was customarily used for that meaning, namely, "epeita," "afterwards." This is the word used in this very passage, in the 23rd verse, where the interval between Christ's resurrection and the resurrection of the righteous saints is mentioned. In a similar way Paul described his visits in Gal. 1:21, "afterwards I came into the regions, etc." We must conclude, then, that there is no justification from its use in the New Testament, for translating "eita" in any other way than as "then," or "next," implying that what follows, follows almost at once. Nor can it be argued that it always refers to the next event of a similar kind, so that there might be a long interval involved because there was no other similar event before the 1000 years were ended, for in three of the events listed in these passages, Luke 8:12, Jn. 20:27, and I Tim. 3:10, the events are different in kind from what preceded.

In the case of the other word in question, "telos," which is translated "end," we find that it is used in the New Testament 42 times. In 35 of these instances it undoubtedly means "end," "limit," or "conclusion," as "he that endureth to the end shall be saved" (Matt. 24:13), or the "end of the age." In three places it means "end" in the sense of "purpose." In one case it is doubtful whether it means "end" in the sense of "purpose," or "end" in the sense of "limit." In three places the word "telos" means "custom" or "impost duty." As we examine the various uses of the word in the New Testament, we find that there is no other place in the New Testament where the word could possibly mean "rest" or "remainder" as Alexander Reese in his book, *The Approaching Advent of Christ,* says it means in this passage in I Cor. 15:24, which we have included among the 35 instances, where it means "end" in the sense of "conclusion." In the passage we are considering, the natural meaning that would suggest itself is that of "end of the age," or, in conjunction with the following words, "end of Christ's kingdom." It is very doubtful whether Paul is considering the resurrection of the wicked dead at all in this whole passage, for as we have said, the subject of discussion is whether the righteous dead will be raised. He is not discussing at all what happens to the wicked dead, (unless he is referring to them in this passage), but is proving that the righteous will rise in spiritual bodies in opposition to the views of the Sadducees or others who denied that there would be any resurrection of the saints. To attempt to find the resurrection of the wicked referred to in the use of the word "telos," "end," is making the wish the father of the thought, and reading into the passage that which is not there. The only natural interpretation of the passage is that the same age in which the dead are raised with glorified bodies, comes to an end when Christ delivers up His kingdom to the Father. The reason the judgment of the wicked is not specifically mentioned here is that he assumes the readers will know that Christ comes to judge all men, living and dead, righteous and wicked, and that the mention of the resurrection of the righteous involves in it the fact of the resurrection of the wicked at the same time, to be judged and sentenced to eternal punishment almost simultaneously. The next event of importance follows immediately, in the turning over of the kingdom to God.

In an attempt to avoid the argument given above, some premillennialists have tried to show that the word "telos," "end" is to
be taken in the sense of "end times," thus applying the word to the
whole period from the beginning to the end of the millennium,
somewhat as the words "last days" or "last hour" are used in
Scripture. An examination of the 42 instances of the use of
"telos" in the New Testament, shows that in no instance is it
used in the sense of "end times," or " last days," but always in
the senses mentioned above, particularly with the meaning, "the
point which marks the limit or conclusion or end of a period or
series of events." It is *never* used elsewhere to cover an extended
period, but always for the end point at the *conclusion* of such an
extended period. Were it not that their theory demands such an
interpretation, no one would dream of reading it into the passage
before us.

As we continue our examination of this passage, we find another
indication that the kingdom of Christ mentioned is the present
kingdom of Christ, not the alleged future millennial kingdom.
Notice the words, "when he shall have overthrown all rule and
all authority and power." These words indicate that the turning
over of the kingdom to the Father follows immediately after the
abolishment of all earthly power. When does that happen? At
the time of the sheep and goat judgment when the wicked nations
are all sent to eternal fire! Jesus said that in the "resurrection
from the dead" there will be no marriage, and of course no births,
so of course since the people will be like the angels, after that time
there will be no authority or power over men but that of Christ
and the Father, after the sheep and goat judgment. The inference
is therefore inescapable, is it not, that the kingdom is then turned
over to the Father? This conclusion is reinforced by the following
words, "For he must reign until he has put all his enemies under
his feet, and the last enemy to be overthrown is death." The period
of reign lasts until the enemies are all subdued, but that happens
at the time of the sheep and goat judgment, so the reigning must
precede that judgment! In other words the present time, the time

when Christ said he has all authority and power, (Matt. 28:18), must be the time of Christ's kingdom.

It cannot be replied that the last enemies are not subdued until the loosing of Satan at the close of the millennium, for that assumes the thing to be proved, namely that that passage in Rev. 20:8-9 refers to the close of the millennium instead of, (as the amillennialist believes), to the period *preceding* the judgment of the sheep and the goats. On premillennial assumptions the living wicked nations are all to be sent to eternal fire when Christ comes at the judgment of the sheep and the goats, while according to Christ's own words there will be no marriage after the resurrection of the righteous, so there would be no births, and therefore no wicked for Satan to gather at the close of the alleged millennium.

But the strongest argument of all is in the words, "The last enemy that shall be abolished is death." The main subject under discussion is the resurrection of believers. When he says that, "the last enemy to be abolished is death," he certainly does not have in mind the resurrection of the wicked, for as far as they are concerned, *death is not an enemy of Christ to be vanquished, but an ally to support!* The abolishment of death as an enemy can only have a reference to the swallowing up of death in victory, mentioned in verse 54. The time of that event is clearly stated to be when believers are transfigured at the coming of Christ. Therefore the abolishment of the last enemy is at *that* time when Christ comes again, and the reign of Christ is therefore "until" that time! The time when the kingdom is turned over to the Father is immediately following, thus leaving no time for an earthly millennial kingdom.

In verse 27, "For He put all things in subjection under His feet," the verb "put" is the past tense, thus indicating that the subjecting of all things to Christ had already taken place when the apostle was writing. This agrees with the words of Jesus, "all authority *has* been given unto me in heaven and on earth." This shows that Christ is ruling at the present time, and indicates that we are not to look for a further millennial reign following the subjection of the last enemy, death, at the resurrection of the righteous. The resurrection of the wicked would naturally be at the same time when death is abolished.

I Corinthians 15:50-54.

"Now this I say, brethren, that flesh and blood cannot inherit the kingdom of God; neither doth corruption inherit incorruption. Behold I show you a mystery; We shall not all sleep, but we shall all be changed in a moment, in the twinkling of an eye, at the last trump; for the trumpet shall sound, and the dead shall be raised incorruptible, and we shall be changed. For this corruptible must put on incorruption and this mortal must put on immortality. But when this corruptible shall have put on incorruption, and this mortal shall have put on immortality, then shall be brought to pass the saying that is written, 'Death is swallowed up in victory.'"

The subject which the apostle is here discussing is the state of believers in the kingdom of God. He does not speak of the millennial kingdom of Christ, but of the kingdom of God, apparently referring to the eternal kingdom of God the Father to which he has already referred in verse 24. He declares that the glorification of believers occurs at the time when "death is swallowed up in victory," a reference to Is. 25:8, admitted by all to be a prophecy of the inauguration of the theocratic reign of Jehovah Messiah. This is at the time of the "last trump," when the dead are raised incorruptible. This is the same time as that referred to in I Thes. 4:13-18, when the rapture of believers occurs, and therefore it is at the inauguration of the kingdom, whether that kingdom be eternal or millennial.

The first thing to be noticed about this passage is that it is in entire agreement with what Jesus said about the future age, namely, that those who enter it will have spiritual bodies, like the angels. (Luke 20:34-36). If the time referred to is the eternal kingdom of God as the amillennialist believes, then that is the final state of believers. On the other hand, if it is a reference to an alleged millennial kingdom, then it asserts that all those, Jews and Gentiles, who "inherit the kingdom of God" that follows the resurrection of the righteous, will have glorified bodies. There is no room here for the assertion that the Jews will enter the millennial kingdom with mortal bodies, for "flesh and blood cannot inherit the kingdom of God." This cannot refer to the church as distinct from the Jewish remnant, for according to the premillennialists those Jews decidedly do "inherit the kingdom." Anyone, Jew or Gentile, who inherits this kingdom in the text, following immediately upon the resurrection of the righteous, will be like the angels in heaven. There is no room for unsaved people in that kingdom, for they will not be present in mortal bodies. Whoever is present will have immortal and incorruptible bodies. There will be no people there whom Satan could deceive at the end of the alleged millennium.

Now notice the phrase, "the last trump." It is clearly the trumpet referred to in Matt. 24:31 when Christ comes on the clouds of heaven and all the tribes of the earth mourn. It is also apparently identical with the trumpet of Is. 27:13, when the outcasts are gathered from Assyria and Egypt to worship Jehovah in His holy mountain, if this verse has an eschatological meaning. Premillennialists place this at the beginning of the millennial kingdom, and it is quite clear that at least it is not at the *close* of any millennial kingdom, though of course it may be at the beginning of the *eternal* kingdom of God, as the amillennialists claim. At any rate this is followed by the glorification of believers, according to the Corinthian passage, while the premillennialists claim that the Isaiah passage is followed by the earthly Jewish kingdom, in which the Jews have mortal bodies. If these trumpets are the same, it is an additional reason for feeling that there must be another than literal interpretation of the Old Testament prophecies. But the important point to which we wish to call attention is the fact that this is the *last* trump. There is apparently to be no other trump at a later time. Now doubtless it might be replied that God could raise the wicked without the use of a trumpet at the close of the millennium, but is there not implied in the connotation of this word "last," the thought that *all* the dead are to be wakened at the sound of the last trumpet? Is not this the same as the resurrection of John 5:28-29, where *all* that are in the tombs shall hear his voice and come forth, they that have done good unto the resurrection of life and they that have done evil unto the resurrection of judgment?" The last trumpet would seem to imply that every single one of the dead answer it without delaying a thousand years.

I Thessalonians 4:13-18.

"But we would not have you ignorant, brethren, concerning them that fall asleep; that ye sorrow not, even as the rest, who have no hope. For if we believe that Jesus died and rose again, even so them also that are fallen asleep in Jesus will God bring with him. For this we say unto you by the word of the Lord, that we that are alive, that are left unto the coming of the Lord, shall in no wise precede them that are fallen asleep. For the Lord himself shall descend from heaven, with a shout, with the voice of the archangel, and with the trump of God: and the dead in Christ shall rise first; then we that are alive, that are left, shall together with them be caught up in the clouds, to meet the Lord in the air: and so shall we ever be with the Lord. Wherefore comfort one another with these words."

In this passage the subject of discussion is as to what will happen to the dead in Christ when Christ comes. The people of Thessalonica had lost loved ones who were believers, and they were worried about them. They expected Christ to come at any time, but they feared that those who had died would not share in the glory of that coming. Paul writes this passage to reassure them. When Christ comes again he will bring the souls of believers with him, and their bodies will be raised from the dead, by the shout, the voice of the archangel and the sound of the trumpet. In verse 15 he says that we believers who are alive will not be raptured before the others, but that the "dead in Christ shall rise first, then we that are alive will be caught up in the clouds together with them, to meet the Lord in the air." Nothing is said about what happens to the bodies of unbelievers other than that they have no hope (verse 13). If they are to be raised at all the natural assumption would be that they would be raised when the dead hear his voice and live.

Most premillennialists, however, declare that the words, "the dead in Christ shall rise first," is a contrast, not between the dead believers and the living believers, but between the dead believers and the dead unbelievers! We submit, however, that such an interpretation is an arbitrary wresting of the text. The phrase "together with them" in the following verse, would lose its meaning if the thought of unbelievers were intruded in the word "first." As these verses read, the interpretation is perfectly simple and natural that the dead believer is raised first, then the living believers with the dead and risen ones go up in the clouds together, the "first" being used to compare the rising of the believer and the rapture of the living believer with him. Any other interpretation is forced and illogical. But not only does this passage teach the resurrection of believers, and their rapture with the living believers; it also teaches that after the rapture they will never be separated from the Lord. Many premillennialists declare that the church is to be left in heaven during the millennium, while Christ reigns in Jerusalem over the Jews, thus separating the the church from Christ. Some premillennialists would declare that the glorified believers could doubtless visit Jerusalem, but their home would really be in heaven. This passage in Thessalonians teaches that whatever happens to Christ, wherever He is, there are the believers. Notice also that there is nothing secret about this rapture. It is accompanied by a shout, the voice of an archangel, and the trumpet of God. It would be hard to keep the event secret,

In the following chapter, Chapter 5, Paul goes on to say that the coming of the day of the Lord will be as sudden and unexpected as the coming of a "thief in the night!" (I Thes. 5:2). Destruction suddenly comes on the wicked at that time, and they shall not escape it. Then Paul goes on to say that believers are not to be overtaken that day as a thief, for they are children of the light, and should live soberly, for God has not appointed us to wrath. This whole passage is directly against the claims of the pretribulationists who claim that the "day of the Lord" is seven years after the rapture, for in this passage it is assumed that the day will be the same for both believers and unbelievers, that they will be together then but that believers will not be overtaken unexpectedly as a thief for they are ready for it by watching and sobriety. Moreover taken in connection with the verses immediately preceding in the 4th chapter, this argument is conclusive. All admit that that chapter deals with the rapture but pretribulationists place this before the tribulation. However, Chapter 5, verse one says, "But concerning the times and the seasons. . . .yourselves know perfectly that the day of the Lord cometh as a thief in the night," thus assuming that the day of the Lord is the day of rapture. No other interpretation seems possible.

II Thessalonians 1:7-10.

"And to you that are afflicted rest with us, at the revelation of the Lord Jesus from heaven with the angels of His power in flaming fire, rendering vengeance to them that know not God, and to them that obey not the gospel of our Lord Jesus: who shall suffer punishment, even eternal destruction from the face of the Lord and from the glory of his might, when he shall come to be glorified in his saints and to be marvelled at in all them that believed, (because our testimony unto you was believed) in that day."

This is a terrible picture of judgment, similar in almost every respect to the judgment of the great white throne of Rev. 20, and to the judgment of the sheep and the goats, as well as similar to the judgment of the tares in the parable of the wheat and the tares. However in this passage the time of the judgment is definitely fixed as that "at the revelation of the Lord Jesus from heaven," "when he comes to be glorified in his saints." In other words, this identifies the time of the judgment with the time of the glorification of Christ in his saints. To make this more plain, it is the time when the believers will marvel at Christ in His beauty. This is directly against the view of the pretribulationists that the coming of Christ is at the beginning of the tribulation while the revelation of the Lord is at its close. This passage declares that the judgment occurs at the time of the coming, the glorification and the marvelling! That is to say all these events are at the same time according to this passage. But if this is at the beginning of an alleged millennium, then notice that *all* unbelievers and all disobedient Christians will be sent to eternal punishment "when he shall come to be glorified in his saints." That means that there will be no disobedient (to the gospel) Jews left on earth afterward. Nor will there be any of the unbelieving nations left to go into an alleged millennium. Moreover, all believers will share in that glorification, and all will be raptured according to the I Thes. 4:13-18 passage, so that there would be no unbelievers left at the end of an alleged millennium for Satan to gather to war against the saints.

Nor is it possible for the premillennialists to claim that this judgment scene is at the *close* of the alleged millennium, for the time is definitely fixed at the coming and revelation of Christ from heaven, while the premillennialist says that Christ is on earth during the 1000 years. The premillennialist is therefore forced by his own assumptions to place this judgment at the beginning of the alleged millennium, but if he does, he is then forced to admit that all the living wicked are sent to eternal destruction *at that time,* while there would be no way others could be born with mortal bodies, since all believers are "like the angels in heaven" after this time, having been glorified. This in turn forces the conclusion that Rev. 20:8-10 must be located before the coming of Christ.

II Thessalonians 2:1-10.

"Now we beseech you, brethren, touching the coming of our
Lord Jesus Christ, and our gathering together unto him, to the
end that ye be not quickly shaken from your mind, nor yet be
troubled, either by spirit or by word, or by epistle as from us as
that the day of the Lord is just at hand: for it will not be except
the falling away come first, and the man of sin be revealed, the son
of perdition, he that opposeth and exalteth himself against all that
is called God or that is worshipped; so that he sitteth in the temple
of God, setting himself forth as God. Remember ye not that when
I was yet with you I told you these things? And ye know now that
which restraineth, to the end that he may be revealed in his own
season. For the mystery of lawlessness doth already work, only
there is one that restraineth now, until he be taken out of the way.
And then shall be revealed the lawless one, whom the Lord Jesus
shall slay with the breath of his mouth and bring to nought by the
manifestation of his coming; even he whose coming is according
to the working of Satan with all power and signs and lying wonders and with all deceit of unrighteousness for them that perish;
because they received not the love of the truth, that they might be
saved."

The passage before us is interesting in a number of respects.
In the first place it declares that the "coming of the Lord," the
"gathering together unto him," and the "day of the Lord" are
declared to be at the same time. In fact the destruction of the
"man of sin" is specifically declared to be at the "manifestation of
his coming." This is directly against the claims of the pretribulationists who say that the coming precedes the day of the Lord
by seven years, and that the man of sin arises *after* the coming of
Christ.

This passage is also directly opposed to the claims of the postmillennialists who claim that the world will get better and better
until the millennium. This declares that there will be a "falling
away," that the man of sin will arise and that he will deceive the

unbelievers before the coming of Christ to destroy him with the breath of His mouth. The world will not all be converted before the coming of Christ, but on the contrary there will be a great apostasy before the coming of Christ.

This passage also teaches that we are not to think that the day of the Lord is just at hand, for we will first see the arising of the man of sin and the great falling away from the church, so that while we may believe in the imminent coming of Christ, we are not to think that it will be before the prophecies about the man of sin, etc., are fulfilled. It is impossible for us to say with any certainty who the one that straineth is, but there would seem to be good reason to believe that it refers to the restraining power of the Holy Spirit in the world, keeping the wicked from being as wicked as they would otherwise be.

II Timothy 4:1, 8, 18.

"I charge thee in the sight of God, and of Christ Jesus, who shall judge the living and the dead, and by his appearing and his kingdom, preach the word....Henceforth there is laid up for me the crown of righteousness, which the Lord, the righteous judge, shall give to me at that day; and not to me only but also to all them that have loved his appearing....The Lord will deliver me from evil work, and will save me unto his heavenly kingdom."

In this passage the appearing of Christ, the kingdom, and the judgment of the living and the dead are all associated together as happening at the same time, as far as one can judge. The kingdom is explained later as the "heavenly kingdom." This can mean only one of two things. Either it refers to the heavenly kingdom of Christ in this present interadventual age, or it refers to the heavenly aspect of the eternal kingdom of Christ and the Father. The qualification of "heavenly" before the kingdom, distinctly teaches that it does *not* refer to a millennial earthly kingdom. In verse 1, if it stood alone, we might find a reference to a 1000 year kingdom, but taken with the explanation in verse 18, we must conclude that the apostle has in mind the same kingdom in verse 1, namely the heavenly kingdom.

Particularly noticeable is the fact that the judgment is of "the living and the dead." This apparently teaches that all, both righteous and unrighteous, whether living or dead, are to be judged at the same time, and associated with the "appearing" of Christ, it would indicate that they are judged at that time.

It is difficult to decide whether "at that day" refers to the judgment day, or to the day Paul will go to heaven, but since it says that God, the *righteous judge* will give this crown of righteousness "at that day," we assume that it happens on the judgment day, when we are made perfectly righteous and glorified.

II Corinthians 5:10.

"For we must all be made manifest before the judgment-seat of Christ; that each one may receive the things done in the body, according to what he hath done, whether it be good or bad."

The Pretribulationists hold that the judgment-seat of Christ is not the judgment of the sheep and the goats, or the great white throne judgment, but that after the rapture of the church before the seven year period of tribulation, the "Bema" or "judgment-seat" of Christ is established in the clouds, and that Christians appear before Christ for the giving of awards.[25] They declare that "Bema" means this judgment seat of Christ in the clouds, not the judgment on earth at the close of the seven year period of tribulation or at the close of the alleged millennium. This argument is based on the fact that the only other place where the word is used in connection with Christ or God is in Rom. 14:10, "For we shall all stand before the judgment-seat of God." In the King James version the words are "judgment-seat of Christ," though the American Revised Version has the correct rendering, "Judgment-seat of God." In the Greek the evidence is so strong for the latter reading that all editors and commentators except the pretribulationists agree that it is correct. The only manuscripts that give "Christ" in place of "God" are late and unreliable. The so-called "Neutral" text is overwhelmingly in favor of the reading, "judgment-seat of God." There is therefore no reason to think that the word teaches anything different from the other judgment passages. It teaches that all men will be judged by Christ or God, since both the Father and the Son agree on all the judgments.

Conclusion.

In our study of the teachings of Paul about "last things," we find that there is no evidence from his writings for any millennium, or for the rapture of the church seven years before the judgment of the sheep and the goats. All the evidence is that the rapture occurs at the time when Christ comes to earth and when all living (at least) men shall be judged at the judgment of the sheep and the goats. There is no reason from the writings of Paul to think that that judgment is not the same as the judgment of the great white throne, and that it is not followed by the eternal kingdom of God.

Chapter XII

THE TEACHING OF PETER ON THE SECOND COMING

II Peter 3:3-13.

"KNOWING this first, that in the last days mockers shall come with mockery, walking after their own lusts, and saying, Where is the promise of His coming? For from the day the fathers fell asleep, all things continue as they were from the beginning of the creation. For this they wilfully forget, that there were heavens from of old, and an earth compacted out of water and amidst water, by the word of God: by which means the world that then was being overflowed with water, perished: but the heavens that now are and the earth by the same word have been stored up for fire, being reserved against the day of judgment and destruction of ungodly men. But forget not this one thing, beloved, that one day is with the Lord as a thousand years, and a thousand years as one day. The Lord is not slack concerning his promise, as some count slackness; but that all should come to repentance. But the day of the Lord will come as a thief; in the which the heavens shall pass away with a great noise and the elements shall be dissolved with fervent heat, and the earth and the works that are therein shall be burned up. Seeing that these things are thus all to be dissolved, what manner of persons ought ye to be in all holy living and godliness, looking for and earnestly desiring the coming of the day of God, by reason of which the heavens being on fire shall be dissolved, and the elements shall melt with fervent heat? But according to his promise, we look for new heavens and a new earth wherein dwelleth righteousness."

110

There can be no doubt from this passage that Peter did not look for the conversion of the world before Christ comes. He teaches definitely that in the last days there will be those who scoff at the promise of Christ's return. Then, too, it is noticeable that the "day of the Lord" and the "day of God," are apparently the same, for on both days it is said that the elements shall be dissolved with fervent heat, followed at once by the new heavens and the new earth in which dwelleth righteousness. The time when this occurs is at the time of the day of judgment and "destruction of ungodly men." Certainly this implies that it will be the judgment of the men who are then living, whatever may be said about the wicked dead. If so then it will be at the beginning of the alleged millennium, for that is when the premillennialists say that the judgment of the living wicked is to occur. Certainly that is when "the day of the Lord comes as a thief." In *that very day,* which is in other Scripture identified with the Second Coming of Christ, (I Thes. 5:2; 5:4; Rev. 3:3; 16:15), Peter tells us that "the earth and the works that are therein shall be burned up!" That does not look very much like the inauguration of a Jewish kingdom which Jews enter in their natural bodies, together with unregenerate Gentile nations over whom Christ reigns with a rod of iron! If they are all burned up, where would men in natural sinful bodies then come from to inhabit the alleged millennial kingdom?

Moreover, Peter tells us that we should be *looking for* and "earnestly desiring the coming of the day of God, by reason of which . . . the elements shall melt with fervent heat!" It would be difficult indeed to think that this time would be at the *end* of the millennium, for how could we "look for" a day if we know that there will be at least 1000 years before its coming? We would know that none of us would live to see that day, so we could not look for it to come, as we *can* look for the coming of Christ, in our own life time.

All these difficulties instantly disappear if we believe that when Christ comes, the dead are all raised, the righteous raptured, the wicked destroyed by fire, the great judgment occurs, and the new heavens and new earth follow immediately. This whole passage in Peter fits in perfectly with this amillennial view. The assumption in the whole passage is that Christ is coming again (verse 4), that the judgment day follows at once, at which time the world and the works that are in it are to be burned up (verses 7, 10, 12), to be followed at once by the new heavens and the new earth (verse 13).

Chapter XIII

HEBREWS, JAMES AND JUDE ON THE SECOND COMING

Hebrews 1:8.

"**B**UT of the Son he saith, Thy throne, O God, is forever and ever; And the sceptre of uprightness is the sceptre of thy kingdom."

Here the Ps. 14:6 passage is quoted with the interpretation that it is concerned with the kingdom of Christ, the Son of God, thus claiming, not a thousand year reign for Him but an *eternal* reign. The symbol of His reign is to be uprightness. This would imply that Christ's reign is now, and on into eternity, though as I Corinthians 15:24 shows, in one sense He turns over his power to the Father at the time of the Second Coming and the resurrection.

Hebrews 12:26-29.

"Yet once more will I make to tremble not the earth only, but also the heaven. And this word, Yet once more, signifieth the removing of those things that are shaken, as of things that have been made, that those things which are not shaken may remain. Wherefore, receiving a kingdom that cannot be shaken, let us have grace, whereby we may offer service well-pleasing to God with reverence and awe: for our God is a consuming fire."

Here the author of Hebrews contrasts created things with invisible, spiritual things, particularly the invisible kingdom of God which believers have received. This clearly indicates that the world will be destroyed in the future, together with the created heavens, but that the eternal kingdom which cannot be destroyed will remain. How can there be, then, a millennial kingdom on this present earth, if that earth is to be destroyed at the time when the next eschatological events take place? The reference to God as a consuming fire, certainly is a reference to the way in which God will burn up the wicked and their works when Christ comes again. There seems to be no place here for an earthly millennial kingdom in the future.

James 5:7-8.

"Be patient, therefore, brethren, until the coming of the Lord ....Be ye also patient; establish your hearts: for the coming of the Lord is at hand."

The significance of this reference to the Second Coming of Christ is that it is the earliest reference to it in the New Testament literature, since James was probably the first book written. This shows that this early in church history we find the New Testament church looking for the close approach of the Second Coming. The Christians are to wait patiently for the realization of that hope in its proper time.

Jude 18.

"In the last time there shall be mockers, walking after their own ungodly lusts."

Unless there is a reference to the future judgment in Jude 14-15, this reference in the 18th verse is all that we have in Jude on eschatology. It clearly indicates that there will be an unconverted world in the time preceding the Second Coming of Christ, thus showing the false hope of postmillennialists for a 1000 years of righteousness.

Chapter XIV

THE APOCALYPSE

THE whole book of the Revelation of John is concerned with "the things which must shortly come to pass" (Rev. 1:1), and of course we cannot attempt to give a commentary on it here. We can only attempt to show the general teachings of the book, with the particular passages that concern the differences between the various views of the last things.

The Outline.

The most satisfactory outline of the Book of the Revelation is that which divides the book into seven sections, carrying out the symbolic figure of seven, the symbol of perfection, throughout the book.

I. Letters to the Seven Churches.   Chap. 1-3.
II. The Seven Seals.   Chap. 4-7.
III. The Seven Trumpets.   Chap. 8-11.
IV. The Seven Personages.   Chap. 12-14.
V. The Seven Bowls.   Chap. 15-16.
VI. The Destruction of Babylon, the Beast and False Prophet.   Chap. 17-19.
VII. The Consummation.   Chap. 20-22.

These seven sections, according to this outline, give contemporaneous pictures of the interadventual period, until the last which starts at the birth of Christ and goes on into eternity. That is to say, each of these sections goes back to the birth of Christ and from different angles gives a description of what happens in the period between the birth of Christ and eternity, though in the latter sections principal emphasis is placed on the events at the close of the interadventual period and beyond. This outline thus makes a beautiful structure architecturally, and fits into the other complex yet beautiful symbolism of the book.

Premillennialists, however, who follow this construction of sevens, insist that the last section does not recapitulate previous history, but describes the period *subsequent* to the previous six sections! In other words they would insist that there is a break in the perfect structure of the book which the other outline gives. To depict this graphically the amillennialist describes the book as follows:

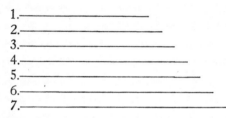

The premillennialist would say that the structure is as follows:

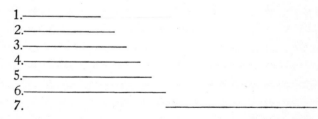

The sixth section either includes the twentieth chapter, or the seventh section begins with the twentieth chapter, but in any case the premillennialist declares that the twentieth chapter describes events that are *subsequent* in time to the events described in the

nineteenth chapter, thus causing a break in the symbolic structure
of the book. In view of the almost geometrical structure of the
book, the outline of the premillennialist would seem to be less
likely to be correct.

There is constant reference to passages in the prophetic books of
the Old Testament throughout Revelation, and the symbolism of
the book is too obvious to need proof. Some of this symbolism is
explained, some of it is obvious, and some of it is obscure and difficult to interpret or understand, but the fact that symbolism is
almost everywhere present in the book, should make one cautious
about insisting on a *literal* interpretation of *any* particular feature
of the book. One of the best commentaries on the book that we
have discovered is the book, *More Than Conquerors,* by W.
Hendriksen, published in 1939. In speaking of the purpose of the
book, Mr. Hendriksen says: "Persecuted believer, this book of
Revelation seeks to impart comfort to you. That is its main purpose: to comfort the militant church in its struggle against the
forces of evil. It abounds with consolations for afflicted believers
....The theme of this book is The Victory of Christ and of His
Church over the Dragon (Satan) and His Helpers. The Apoca-
lypse intends to show you, dear believer, that things are not what
they seem! The beast that comes up out of the abyss *seems* to be
victorious....In reality it is the believer who triumphs." This
description of the book, its purpose and theme, gives us a sane
approach to this whole perplexing question of interpretation of
the book. We also agree with this author when he says that,
"The book owes its origin, at least in part, to contemporary conditions. It is God's answer to the prayers and tears of severely
persecuted Christians scattered about in the cities of Asia Minor.
Nevertheless...we should give equal prominence to the fact that
this book was intended *not only* for those who first read it but for
believers throughout this entire dispensation" (pp. 11, 12, 14,
15). We should bear these points in mind in our attempts to
understand the prophecies about eschatology in this book.

The Kingdom.

Throughout the book references are made to "a kingdom," in which believers have a part here and now, thus lending plausibility to the claims of the amillennialists that the kingdom of Rev. 20 is the same kingdom referred to in other parts of the book, and is the reign of believers with Christ here and now, both on earth and in heaven. Rev. 1:6, "He made us to be a kingdom, priests unto His God and Father," clearly indicates that believers are here and now a kingdom under Christ. John says that he is a partaker of this kingdom. Rev. 1:9, "I, John, your brother and partaker with you in the tribulation and kingdom and patience which are in Jesus," which can only be the present kingdom of Christ. In Rev. 3:21, "He that overcometh, I will give to him to sit down with me in my throne, as I also overcame and sat down with My Father in His throne," indicates that Christ is reigning now, and that the souls of believers who overcome will share in that reign in this dispensation in heaven. In Rev. 5:10, we are told that redeemed Christians were purchased by Christ and that He "madest them to be unto our God a kingdom and priests; and they reign upon the earth." There is a serious question as to whether the text here should read, "they shall reign," or "they reign," but even though the future reading be accepted as correct, there is no question about the tense of the previous verb, so that it would mean that Christ has made Christians a kingdom already, and that they will continue to reign upon the earth in the future, thus giving no grounds for thinking that it refers to an alleged millennial kingdom. These many references to the fact that believers are now reigning with Christ both on earth and in heaven, give additional weight to the belief that the same inter-adventual reign is referred to in Rev. 20, and not an alleged millennial reign.

Christ's Coming.

It is particularly noteworthy that while in Rev. 1:7 John says, "Behold he cometh with the clouds; and every eye shall see him, and they that pierced him; and all the tribes of the earth shall mourn over him," thus indicating that His coming will be public and will be accompanied by the judgment, in Rev. 16:15, we read, "To gather them together unto the war of the great day of God, the Almighty, (Behold I come as a thief. Blessed is he that watcheth and keepeth his garments, lest he walk naked, and they see his shame). And they gathered them together into the place which is called in Hebrew Armageddon" (Rev. 16:14-16). The pretribulationists insist that the "coming as a thief" is at the time of the rapture *before* the Great Tribulation, and that the battle of Armageddon is at the close of the tribulation period. In this passage, however, the "war of the great day of God" certainly must refer to the judgment, and the terrible vengeance inflicted on unbelievers at the battle of Armageddon, yet in the center of the passage dealing with that vengeance, it is inserted that Christ comes as a thief and believers are warned to watch for him *at that time*. This is directly against the pretribulation view of Christ's coming.

The First Resurrection.

We must now discuss one of the cornerstone claims of the premillennialists, that there are two resurrections separated by the millennium.[26] The first resurrection is held to be the resurrection of the righteous at the time of Christ's Second Coming, while the second resurrection is claimed to be at the close of the alleged millennium and for the wicked only. This argument is based on Rev. 20:5, "The rest of the dead lived not until the thousand years should be finished. This is the first resurrection. Blessed and holy is he that hath part in the first resurrection: over these the second death hath no power; but they shall be priests of God and of Christ, and shall reign with him a thousand years." The amillennialist however believes that the first resurrection is the new birth of the believer which is crowned by his being taken to heaven to be with Christ in His reign during the interadventual period. This eternal life which is the present possession of the believer, and is not inter-

rupted by death of the body, is the first resurrection and partici-
pation in it is the millennial reign.

In John 5:24-29 we have the two resurrections brought together
in the same paragraph. "He that heareth my word, and believeth
him that sent me, hath eternal life, and cometh not into judgment,
but hath passed out of death into life. Verily, verily, I say unto
you, the hour cometh and now is, when the dead shall hear the
voice of the Son of God; and they that hear shall live. . . . Marvel
not at this: for the hour cometh in which all that are in the tombs
shall hear His voice, and shall come forth; they that have done
good, unto the resurrection of life; and they that have done evil,
unto the resurrection of judgment." Now though the word "first
resurrection" is not used in this paragraph, clearly the fact is taught
inescapably. What else can we call passing "out of death into life,"
but resurrection? Notice that it is contrasted with the resurrection
which takes place when the dead bodies of all men are raised. Notice also that it is said that *all* that are in the tombs shall hear the
voice of Christ and come forth. Then, as they come forth from the
tombs, the separation takes place into the resurrection of life and
the resurrection of judgment. The use of these two terms, "resurrection of life" and "resurrection of judgment" in connection with
the previous statement that *all* hear Christ's voice and come forth
for the separation into the resurrection of life and the resurrection
of judgment, in no way indicates a separation in time of a thousand
years, as the premillennialist claims, for it distinctly says that *all*,
good and bad, hear the voice and come forth.

In Daniel 12:1-2, we have another reference to the resurrection.
"And there shall be a time of trouble, such as never was since there
was a nation even to that same time: and at that time thy people
shall be delivered, every one that shall be found written in the
book. And many of them that sleep in the dust of the earth shall
awake, some to everlasting life, and some to shame and everlasting
contempt." The time of trouble here referred to coincides with the
Great Tribulation, At that time, the time of deliverance of those
written in the book, (clearly the book of life), is the time when

many of the dead are raised from "the dust of the earth." The use of the "many," in no way helps the premillennialist, for it says that part of those raised from the dead awake to everlasting life, while others awake to everlasting contempt. The resurrection here mentioned clearly takes place at the close of the tribulation period, and just as clearly is a resurrection of both righteous and wicked at the same time. However the use of the word "many" of the dead may be explained, the premillennialists do not claim that *some* of the righteous are raised at the beginning of the alleged millennium and others at the close of it, but that *all* the wicked are raised at the close of the millennium, while *all* the righteous are raised at the beginning of the alleged millennium. This passage clearly teaches that the good and the wicked are raised together. Probably the use of the word "many" is explained by the fact that the prophet saw a great multitude, "many," raised, and cautiously refrained from claiming that all were raised. There would be no contradiction however between that and the passages that teach that all the dead are to be raised. There is no warrant here for claiming that there are to be two bodily resurrections separated by a thousand years.

In Acts 25:15, "That there shall be a resurrection both of the just and unjust," is another passage in which the resurrection of both the righteous and the wicked is assumed to occur at the same time. The only fair interpretation of the passage is that there is no separation in time between the resurrection of the just and the unjust. The passage says that there is to be, not two resurrections, but a resurrection, and that in the resurrection there will be two classes of people, unjust and just. How could the author have expressed the thought more clearly?

Now the first resurrection, as the resurrection of the soul dead in sin to eternal life in Christ, who is "the resurrection and the life," is called, is taught in many passages of the New Testament. In Romans 6:4-6 the resurrection of Christ is compared with the "walk in newness of life," and the union of the believer with Christ through faith is spoken of in Rom. 6:5 as being "also in the likeness of His resurrection." What can the likeness of the resurrection of Christ possibly be but also resurrection? In Rom. 6:13 Christians are urged to present themselves to God as "alive from the dead," thus calling the new birth a resurrection from the dead. In Col. 2:12 the same truth is taught in very significant language: "Wherein ye were also raised with Him through faith in the working of God, who raised Him from the dead." Our new birth is here directly called being "raised" with Christ. The same truth is taught in Col. 3:1, "If ye then were raised together with Christ, seek the things that are above, where Christ is, seated on the right hand of God." The new birth is thus a resurrection just as the resurrection of Christ was a resurrection, and we are to join with Christ in His reign seated on the right hand of God. In Eph. 2:4, "Made us alive together with Christ," and Eph. 5:14, "Awake thou that sleepest and arise from the dead, and Christ shall shine upon thee," it is clearly taught that the new birth is a resurrection from the dead.

But not only is the new birth called resurrection from the dead or "rising from the dead"; it continues without interruption on into eternity. John 11:25-26, "I am the resurrection and the life: he that liveth and believeth in me shall never die," teaches that once there is new birth, the individual continues alive into eternity. Christ's whole argument with the Jews who denied the doctrine of the resurrection was based on the proof from the Old Testament that God was not "the God of the dead but of the living," (Mark 12:26-27) thus claiming that the persistence of the souls of the patriarchs after death was a resurrection, and proved the doctrine of the resurrection. The first resurrection was from death in sin to life in Christ. The second resurrection will be the quickening of the body as well as the soul. The first resurrection is to *eternal* life (I John 5:11-13), and the subsequent separation of the soul from the body at death is only an incident in that eternal life. When the soul goes to be with Christ in glory, the consummation of the first resurrection is reached, and the soul then reigns with Christ in heaven (Rev. 20:4), in continuation of the reign with Christ which started at the time when he was born again and raised to new life in Christ in the likeness of His resurrection.

It is argued by the premillennialists that there is no warrant for taking the term "first resurrection," in Rev. 20:5, in other than a literal sense as applying to the bodily resurrection, in spite of the constant use of the new birth in the sense of rising from the dead, in the New Testament, as we have already shown. However there is certainly more than a hint in Rev. 20:6 that the "first resurrection" is not to be interpreted literally, in the fact that it is coupled with the "second death," a term which cannot possibly, by any stretch of the imagination, be called literal death. "Blessed and holy is he that hath part in the first resurrection: over these the second death hath no power." The "second death" is the punishment of the individual in eternal punishment, certainly just the opposite of literal death. So if the second death is not literal there is no reason why the first resurrection cannot be the resurrection of the soul to life in Christ. The contrast between the first resurrection and the second death in this verse would lose much of its meaning if one were the literal resurrection of the body and the other the figurative death of the soul and body in the lake of fire. The terrible feature of the "second death" is not the fact that it is the resurrected body that physically suffers eternal punishment in the lake of fire, but that it is the *soul* which is forced to endure such terrible eternal anguish that whether it is a literal lake of fire or the figurative fires of a conscience-stricken soul, in either case the soul suffers eternally. If the "first resurrection" refers to the eternal life of the new-born soul in eternal bliss, reigning with Christ *now,* there is definite point to the contrast with the second death which has no power over such souls reigning with Christ.

The Reign of the Twenty-Four Elders.

"And the seventh angel sounded; and there followed great voices in heaven, and they said:

The kingdom of the world is become the kingdom of
our Lord and of His Christ: and He shall reign forever
and ever!' And the four and twenty elders, who sit before God on their thrones, fell upon their faces and worshipped God, saying,

'We give thee thanks, O Lord God, the Almighty, who art and
who wast; because thou hast taken thy great power, and didst
reign, and the nations were wroth, and thy wrath came, and the
time of the dead to be judged, and the time to give their reward
to thy servants the prophets, and to the saints, and to them that
fear thy name, the small and the great; and to destroy them that
destroy the earth.' " Rev. 11:15-18.

In order to understand this passage, it is necessary to ask ourselves who are the twenty-four elders that sit before God on their
thrones? Are they men or are they angels? Well, there is nothing
about them to indicate that they are superhuman beings. They
appear over and over again through the book, but always around
the throne of God, with golden crowns on their heads, seated on
thrones, or casting their crowns at the feet of the One on the
throne, and falling in worship before Him. They help to interpret the visions to John. The best explanation perhaps of their
identity is that they are the representatives of the Old and New
Dispensations, twelve from each, seen reigning and worshipping
God around His throne. The function of elders both in the Old
and New Testaments was to hold spiritual rule over God's people,
as representatives of the people of God, sharing in the reign with
the Lamb.

If this interpretation is correct, then it is important to notice
the *time* when this reign is taking place. It is *before* the Second
Coming of Christ, not *after* it. In the passage before us it describes
what occurs *after* the seventh trumpet sounds, at the close of the
great tribulation. The twenty-four elders are pictured *already*
seated on thrones, before the throne of God. They are *already*

ruling *before* the seventh trumpet sounds! In other words their reign *precedes* the beginning of the kingdom here pictured! Of course there is nothing to indicate that they stop reigning at this time, but at least they have already been reigning! This would coincide with the picture in Rev. 20:4 of the *souls* reigning with Christ now. The elders would be representative of the great host of the redeemed who reign with Christ in heaven.

But there is another important feature that is to be noted in this picture. The first thing that the great voices say is that the kingdom of the world *is become* the kingdom of the Lord and of His Christ. This can only be the kingdom of the Father, since it is coupled with the words "of His Christ." Instead of introducing a reign of a thousand years, it distinctly says that "He shall reign forever and ever." It begins at the time of the sounding of the seventh trumpet which premillennialists admit is at the close of this dispensation, therefore it rules out any possible millennial reign to follow this dispensation.

But still more important than this is the fact that this is "the time of the dead to be judged." This can only be the great white throne judgment, for according to the premillennial principles the righteous do not enter into judgment, and the wicked are not said to be raised at the time of the judgment of the sheep and the goats. This is further proved by the fact that it is coupled with the words "Thy wrath came." This cannot possibly refer to the righteous, so it must be a reference to the judgment of the great white throne. But if it is, it is clearly at the time which *precedes* the alleged millennium, for it is the same time when rewards are given to the righteous, and the premillennialists claim that that time is *before* the alleged millennium. But it is also at the same time when the living wicked are judged, for the last verse closes with the words, "to destroy them that destroy the earth."

While this whole passage fits perfectly into the amillennial interpretation, with saints reigning now with Christ, the judgment of all men, living and dead, at the one great judgment day, when the kingdoms of this world become the kingdom of God the Father, the whole passage is directly against the premillennial theory, for in this passage the elders reign before the time when the trumpet blows, the kingdom is the kingdom of God, but the time is at the close of the great tribulation, and the judgment of the wicked which must be the great white throne judgment, as we have shown above, occurs when the awards are given to the righteous and when the living wicked are to be judged, so it must be at the time when Christ comes, all these points being contradictory to the premillennial theory.

Alexander Reese, in *The Approaching Advent of Christ*, p. 75, says that the judgment here pictured is only the judgment of the righteous dead, but the only reason he gives for this statement is that "this book (i.e., The Revelation) reveals that the unsaved dead are judged at the conclusion of the Messianic Kingdom, not at its beginning (20:5, 11-14)." But this assumes the very point at issue, namely that the great white throne judgment is at the conclusion of the millennium! Reese himself has claimed that John 5:24 teaches that the believer cometh not into judgment, though he quotes Rom. 14:10-12 and I Cor. 3:13-15 to show that the believer enters into a judgment to determine the reward of each. But notice that the Corinthians passage merely states that our works are to be tested, while the Romans passage states that we shall stand before the judgment seat of God to give account of ourselves to God. As we have already shown, the time when the "dead are judged," according to premillennial principles is at the time of the great white throne judgment, and this judgment is of both good and bad men, that is, to determine whether they are written in the book of life. The phrase, "the time of the dead to be judged," following after the words, "thy wrath came," certainly implies more than simply the award of prizes to those who are saved! The only natural connotation of these words is the judgment of the unbelieving dead at the same time the righteous dead stand before the judgment seat of Christ. In other words, were it not for the assumption that the wicked dead are not judged till the end of the millennium, anyone reading these words, "the time of the dead to be judged," would naturally conclude that it was the time when either *all* the dead, both good and evil, are judged, or that it was the time when the *wicked* dead are to be judged. The whole picture of the first part of the verse is of wrath and condemnation, while the close of the verse is also a picture of wrath and condemnation. In the middle of the verse is the picture of the giving of rewards, thus indicating that the judgment of the wicked dead and the giving of rewards to the righteous are at the same time.

Chapter XV

DOES REVELATION CHAPTER 20 TEACH AN EARTHLY MILLENNIUM?

IN any discussion of eschatology, the premillennialist usually answers most arguments against the premillennial theory by declaring, "But what are you going to do with Revelation 20? It teaches an earthly millennium in the future, and you have no right to spiritualize it away!" It is not too much to say that this chapter is the very citadel of the premillennial system, and the norm to which all other prophetic passages must be made to conform. It is said to teach a thousand year earthly kingdom of Christ in plain language, and though that thousand year earthly kingdom is not found elsewhere in the teachings of Jesus or the Apostles, it must be inserted between the lines, no matter how many contradictions may be produced by doing so. Nowhere else is the idea of two resurrections separated by 1000 years taught, but the other resurrection passages must be torn apart so that this idea can be inserted somewhere. The great white throne judgment must be placed 1000 years after the coming of Christ, because that is where it is said to be taught in this chapter, though all the other judgment passages are said to place the judgment *before* the alleged millennium, and weird difficulties arise by separating these judgments by a thousand years. The wicked dead are said not to be raised until after the alleged millennium, because this chapter is said to demand it, in spite of the fact that the rest of Scripture would seem to teach that they are raised when Christ comes again. Gentile nations of unregenerated people are said to be on earth during the thousand years under the millennial rule of Christ, in spite of the plain teaching of Christ that after He comes again *only* those who have glorified bodies will "attain to the next age," and *they* will be like the angels (Luke 20:24-36), because this chapter in Revelation is said to teach that Satan gathers such wicked nations at the *close* of the alleged millennium! The rest of Scripture is thus forced into conformity with this one chapter, no matter what difficulties of interpretation may arise in such a process.

Now of course we would not imply that any doctrine which is taught in only one chapter of the Bible is therefore to be ruled out as impossible. If these ideas which are said by premillennialists to be taught in the twentieth chapter of Revelation are actually and inescapably taught there, they must be accepted as part of Scriptural truth by those who accept the Bible as the Word of God. However, if the rest of Scripture cannot be fitted into any such millennial picture, and there is a plausible alternative interpretation of Revelation 20 which removes all difficulties of harmonizing the chapter with the rest of Scripture, the presumption would then be strongly against the premillennial interpretation of Revelation 20 being the correct one.

We have already in previous chapters referred again and again to difficulties which arise from the premillennial interpretation of Revelation 20, but in order that our treatment of this chapter may be found in one place, we will be forced to repeat some of our arguments found in other chapters.

We would call attention first of all to the fact that the chapter in question occurs in a book which is highly figurative and symbolical. This fact is self-evident and therefore needs no proof. This does not mean that the facts recorded in this chapter are to be explained away for that reason, but it does mean that we should be on our guard against insisting that a literal or material explanation of various items in the chapter *must* be accepted as necessarily true.

In the second place, the structure of the book, as we have shown in the previous chapter, makes it fall into seven parallel and contemporaneous sections. According to the amillennial interpretation of the chapter, all seven sections begin at the coming of Christ and describe events between the first and second advents of Christ, but lapping over at the end into eternity. According to the premillennial interpretation the first six sections are parallel and contemporaneous, while the seventh, beginning with Chapter 20, instead of being parallel and contemporaneous with the other six sections, and like the others, starting with the first coming of Christ and going on into eternity, takes up its description of time *subsequent* to the time recorded in the sixth section, thus breaking the harmonious geometrical structure of the book.

According to the premillennial interpretation of Rev. 20, at the end of the present church age Satan is to be bound during the thousand year reign of Christ on earth after His Second Coming. During that millennial reign certain classes of people are to reign with Christ. (Premillennialists usually insist that the Jews reign with Christ over the Gentile nations,[27] though this chapter states that the souls of those beheaded for the testimony of Jesus and for the Word of God, and such as worshipped not the beast neither his image and received not his mark on their forehead and upon their hand reigned with Christ a thousand years. Premillennialists are not united on the point as to who reigns during the thousand years.)   At the close of the thousand year period Satan is to be loosed and is to gather the nations to war against the saints. Fire comes down from heaven and devours them. Satan is then to be cast into the lake of fire, the second resurrection, that of the wicked, takes place and the judgment of the Great White Throne follows. The wicked are then cast into hell, and the eternal kingdom of God is set up on earth and in heaven.

The amillennialist, on the other hand, says that the 20th chapter of Revelation begins with events which occurred shortly after the First Advent of Christ, and describes events in the interadventual period as do the previous six sections of Revelation. Let us now examine the chapter and see whether such an interpretation is possible and plausible.

The first event mentioned is the binding of Satan. If the chapter describes events in the interadventual period, then we ought to find something connected with the ministry of Christ which would fit in with the "binding of Satan." If we turn to Matthew 12:24-29, we find exactly such an event as we are searching for. The Pharisees charged that Jesus was casting out demons by the power of Beelzebub the prince of demons. Jesus replied that if that were the case, Satan's kingdom would be divided against itself, but if He by the power of the Spirit of God cast out demons, then the kingdom of God was come upon them. He then went on to explain that no one can spoil the house of a strong man without first *binding the master of the house!* The context makes it perfectly plain that Christ was claiming that he could cast out demons because he had first *bound* Satan! Here then we have definite authority in the words of Jesus Himself, for saying that He had "bound" Satan before casting out demons. How was that possible? By his resisting all the temptations of Satan in the wilderness and all through His life; by His bearing the penalty due to His people, and thus setting them free in principle from the bondage of Satan; by His rising from the dead and breaking the power of death itself; by all these things, but particularly by *opening the way of salvation to the Gentiles* who dwelt in the power of darkness, under the deception of Satan, and making it impossible for him to deceive them any longer, as to the way of salvation. Before the coming of Christ the nations of the world could only come to God through becoming Jews. We may say that they were universally under the deception and domination of Satan. That deceptive power of Satan was destroyed in principle by Jesus' life and death and resurrection, and the Gentiles "saw a great light."

I suppose that no one would insist that Satan is to be bound with a literal chain of iron or some other metal, for Satan is a spirit and material chains could not hold him captive for a moment. Binding always means the limitation of power in some way. When men bound themselves with an oath not to do something, they agreed to limit their own power and rights to the extent of their oaths. A man and wife are bound by their marriage vows, but that does not mean that they are bound in respect to other relationships in life. A slave is bound to his master, but he lives his life as a human being with freedom to do countless other things which do not interfere with his relationship as a slave to his master. So Satan's being bound does not mean that he is powerless to tempt people, and we know that he does. It is merely limitation of Satan's power in one particular respect especially, that of ability to "deceive the nations." During the interadventual period the gospel is to be proclaimed to all nations, and Satan is powerless to prevent it. The way of salvation has been opened to all nations and there is nothing that Satan can do to block that way.

This idea of the limitation of Satan's power through the work of Christ, is repeatedly taught in the New Testament. In Colossians 2:14-15 we read, "having blotted out the bond written in ordinances that was against us, which was contrary to us: and he hath taken it out of the way, nailing it to the cross; *having despoiled the principalities and powers,* he made a show of them openly, triumphing over them in it." The principalities and powers can only be the powers of Satan, and Paul here declares that Christ has despoiled Satan, made a show of him openly, and triumphed over him. This certainly means that He has limited Satan's powers.

In John 12:31, "Now is the judgment of this world; now shall the *prince of this world be cast out,"* Jesus declares that then, during His earthly life, the devil was to be cast out, defeated by the Son of God in the conflict in which they were engaged. Certainly this was limiting the power of Satan.

In Hebrews 2:14, the writer tells us, "that through death He might *bring to nought* him that had the power of death, that is, the devil." Christ brought the devil to nought, that is, He limited the devil's power in such a way that all his efforts amounted to nothing, and his power was definitely frustrated. All these things show that in the New Testament Christ claimed that in a very real sense he had bound Satan, and limited his power. In Revelation 20, one particular aspect of that binding is before us, namely the limiting of Satan's power to deceive the nations as he did before the coming of Christ. From that time forward during the whole of the interadventual dispensation Satan is defeated in principle, and in regard to that national deception, is defeated in fact. He can still go about like a roaring lion seeking whom he may devour, but in this particular respect he is a caged lion.

But in the end time "Satan is to be loosed for a little time" to deceive the nations again and to gather them to war against the saints. That is, he will be able to stop the preaching of the gospel in the ends of the earth, and will again be able to control the thinking of the nations so that they become his willing dupes to believe a lie. As we look about us at the world to-day, who can say that we are not perhaps entering on the period of such deception of the nations? Who would have dreamed twenty years ago that the whole of Europe could be brought under the control of one man, Hitler, in the short space of ten years? As we see Russia and China under the Soviet despots crushing out true Christianity, is this not almost national deception? Whether this be the time prophesied in the twentieth of Revelation or not, the view that such a time of national Satanic deception will come before Christ comes again, does not seem, in the light of recent international events, so preposterous as it might have seemed forty years ago.

The next item of note in this twentieth chapter is in verse four: "I saw *souls* . . . and they lived and reigned with Christ a thousand years." This word "soul," is "pseuke" in the Greek. It is used 105 times in the New Testament, and in 100 places unquestionably means the soul of man as distinct from his body. In the remaining five instances, one of which is Rev. 20:4, there is a question as to whether the body is referred to as well as the soul. In the following verse, verse 5, the "first resurrection" is mentioned, and the soul living and reigning with Christ, mentioned in verse four, is said to be the "first resurrection." As we have already seen, Scripture gives many precedents for believing that the first resurrection is the new birth which reaches its culmination and consummation when the soul of the believer leaves the body and goes to reign with Christ in heaven. The deliberate choice of the word "soul," which almost universally means soul as distinct from body, as applying to the believers now reigning with Christ in glory, seems to make it perfectly plain that the first resurrection is just that. If it were the literal resurrection of the body, why should the author choose a word which almost always does *not* mean body? Isn't that a definite indication that it is the disembodied spirit that is reigning with Christ? In other words, does this not refer to the "blessed dead who die in the Lord, from henceforth " (Rev. 14:13), who are now present with Christ and reigning with Him in the reign of which He said, "All authority hath been given unto me in heaven and on earth"?

The thousand years would then refer to the perfect cycle of events between the two comings of our Lord. It has two aspects: the first aspect is on earth where Satan is bound so that he can no longer deceive the nations. "The gates of hell shall not prevail against the church " (Matt. 16:18). Until the end of this dispensation, the gospel will be preached to the ends of the earth, and all nations shall see and know the way of salvation, though they may spurn it and reject the Saviour. Satan cannot prevent the nations from seeing the light of the Gospel in the face of Jesus Christ. God's people are a "royal priesthood" here and now, and they are citizens of heaven, their true home. They reign in Christ from the moment they enter into eternal life. But the other aspect of their reign for the thousand year perfect cycle between the two comings, is in heaven, where the glorious aspect of the millennial reign is manifest. We have a picture of that glorious reign in the

passages about the four and twenty elders whose thrones are before the throne of Christ, and who worship the Lamb in company
with the angels. In this twentieth chapter of Revelation we are told
that the souls of all believers share in that glorious millennial reign
up till Christ comes. What a comfort this is for those whose loved
ones have gone on before! We can rejoice in their happiness when
we realize that they are reigning in heaven with Christ here and
now!

There is additional proof that this is the correct interpretation,
in the words in verse 5, "the rest of the dead," indicating that the
ones just mentioned belong to the category of the dead, but their
spirits have been resurrected in the first resurrection, the new
birth bringing eternal life, culminating in that glorious entrance
into heaven at death. The rest of the dead are in hopeless darkness, without eternal life, and when their bodies are raised after
Christ comes, it is only to "shame and everlasting contempt."

Now notice that the idea of our reigning *now* with Christ on
earth is a common one in the New Testament. In Rom. 5:17 we
read, "Much more shall they that receive the abundance of grace
and of the gift of righteousness *reign* in life, through the one, even
Jesus Christ." The context clearly indicates that this is the present earthly reign with Christ. Similarly in Rom. 5:21, grace is
said to reign now. In II Tim. 2:12, "if we endure, we shall also
reign with him," probably refers to the same earthly reign, though
it is possible that it refers to the heavenly reign with Christ. Even
to claim that it referred to the alleged millennium in the future
would not help the premillennialist, for it is the believers, not the
Jews, who reign with Christ, and the literal interpretation of the
Old Testament prophecies demands that it shall be a *Jewish* kingdom. This same thought of reigning with Christ because of our
present resurrection life, is found in I Peter 2:9, "ye are an elect
race, a royal priesthood, a holy nation." Those who are a royal
priesthood belong to the royal family. Since Christ now is reigning
with the Father at His right hand, we who are the adopted sons

and daughters of God, are joint-heirs to the kingdom and are sharing in His reign. As Paul tells us in Col. 1:13, "God has delivered us out of the power of darkness and translated us into the kingdom of His Son." That kingdom is the present kingdom of Christ, and we reign with him in the spiritual realm now, and continue to reign with him after death in heaven (Rev. 20:4), and will reign with God the Father and Christ the Son throughout all eternity (Rev. 21:7).

But let us continue to examine Rev. 20. In the 8th verse we come to the gathering of Gog and Magog. On premillennial assumptions this is at the *close* of the alleged millennium, but in Ezekiel 39:1 ff. the destruction of Gog and Magog *precedes* the bringing back of the "captivity of Jacob," which premillennialists say is at the beginning of the alleged millennium. How is it possible to reconcile these two pictures on premillennial assumptions? Are we to say that after the destruction of Gog and Magog at the *beginning* of the alleged millennium, another Gog and Magog arise at its close? To all appearances the destruction pictured in both places is the same, while if the interpretation of the promises made to Israel as applying to all true Christians, given by Paul, is accepted, then the picture in both places is the destruction of unbelievers preceding the judgment of the Great White Throne, *at the time* when Christ comes in the clouds, not 1000 years later.

But, as we have already shown, the greatest problem of all for the premillennialist is the loosing of Satan and the gathering of the wicked nations to war against the saints, Rev. 20:7-9. Just who are these saints, anyway, according to premillennial principles? If they are the resurrected and transfigured saints reigning with Christ during the alleged millennium, then they are "a multitude whom no man can number" (Rev. 7:9). The term "saints" is always applied to Christians in the New Testament, and according to premillennial principles the church has already been raptured before the millennium, so all the "saints" would have glorified bodies. Since they are in glorified bodies, how could they be injured by any physical weapon, for there is "no pain" in that state (Is. 35:10; Rev. 21:4; Is. 65:19)? But neither could they be injured by spiritual weapons by Satan and his hosts, for they are sinless and cannot sin then, but are "like the angels in heaven"! But could we say that these "saints" are Jews? It is unbelievable that they should be called "saints" in the New Testament unless they had become Christians. However, even though they were Jews, they could not die or have material bodies according to Jesus, for He said: "They that are accounted worthy to attain to that age . . . are equal unto the angels" (Luke 20:35-36)!

But how could there be any wicked nations for Satan to gather "as the sand of the sea?" According to premillennialists the nations before the millennium were all judged, and therefore must have been destroyed and sent to eternal punishment at the sheep and goat judgment[28] (Matt. 25:46), and all unbelievers and disobedient Jews or disobedient Gentiles were likewise sent into eternal punishment at the time when Christ comes "to be glorified in His saints" (II Thes. 1:10), so there would be no living wicked in the whole earth at the beginning of the alleged millennium. It would be impossible for children to be born during the alleged millennium since all the righteous who enter that age, "neither marry nor are given in marriage, neither can they die any more, but are equal unto the angels" (Luke 20:34-36). Since no wicked nations exist on earth at the beginning of the alleged millennium, having all been sent to eternal punishment; since the righteous cannot fall into sin and cannot bear children; and since the wicked dead have not yet been raised according to the premillennialists, just whom could Satan gather to war against the saints?

Of course we understand very well that Zech. 8:5, and Is. 65:20, if literally interpreted as applying to a future Jewish national restoration, teach that there will be births then, but if that be accepted as literally true, how can it be reconciled with the words of Jesus which we have referred to above, in which He says there will be no marriage during the period following the resurrection from the dead of the righteous? Which is to be our standard? Literal interpretation of Old Testament prophecy, or acceptance of the eschatological teaching of Christ? In view of the fact that the New Testament itself interprets a great many of the Old Testament prophecies in other than a literal way, while a literal interpretation of these prophecies brings them into contradiction with the plain teachings of Christ, is there any doubt as to how we should interpret them?

The true interpretation of Revelation 20:8 is that this war there pictured is the same one as that which occurs before the coming of Christ (Rev. 16:16; 19:11-18). If it is one and the same war, then there is no problem in the chapter, and the earthly millennial kingdom imagined by the premillennialist, vanishes into the realm of dreams. The binding of Satan occurred at the time of Christ's earthly ministry, while the loosing of Satan occurs at the close of the interadventual period. There is one objection that needs to be considered. It is claimed that these two battles cannot be the same for in one it is said that birds eat the flesh of the dead bodies, while in the other that fire devours them. However, if these are not hyperbolic descriptions of the terrible destruction that comes upon the wicked, and they are intended to be taken literally, then there is the possibility that after the fire destroys their lives, the birds eat the charred bodies.

In view of all the other teachings of Scripture, and the many contradictions that would arise from the premillennial interpretation of this 20th chapter of Revelation, is it not reasonable to accept the interpretation which clears up all contradictions and harmonizes with the other teachings of Scripture? According to this view, the whole chapter describes the interadventual period up to and including the final judgment. The millennial kingdom, instead of following the coming of Christ, is a two-fold kingdom in this present age. The earthly phase concerns the church of Christ in the world, in which believers reign with Christ and are free from the bondage to Satan, while at the same time the souls of those who are in glory reign with Christ in heaven, till He comes to raise their dead bodies, and to judge the wicked in the Great Assize before the Great White Throne. This explanation is simple, agrees with the whole teaching of Scripture and is true to the fundamental teachings of the Gospel. On the other hand the premillennial view seems to produce irreconcilable contradictions with the rest of Scripture, as we have previously pointed out.

Moreover it is difficult to see how the theory can escape certain serious charges. In the first place, does not the theory really dishonor Christ, even though such an intention is far from the minds of the advocates of the theory? If the Old Testament prophecies are to be literally interpreted as the advocates of the theory insist, then it must be held that bloody animal sacrifices and circumcision will be reinstituted in connection with worship in the millennial temple! If so, did not Christ die in vain? In the second place, according to those premillennialists who declare that the Holy Spirit is to be withdrawn from the world before the Great Tribulation,[29] men will have to believe through their own power after that, since the Holy Spirit is not present in the world, yet they declare that many will believe the "gospel of the kingdom" during that seven year period. Does not that really dishonor the Holy Spirit, by assuming that His work is after all unnecessary, if men can believe through their own strength though the Word of God teaches that men are dead in trespasses and sins (Eph. 2:1), and men cannot see the kingdom of Heaven unless they are born of the Spirit (John 3:5, 8)? In the third place, those forms of premillennialism which teach that the millennial kingdom was *offered* to the Jews[30] of Christ's day and that when they rejected it, it was withdrawn from them for the duration of the present dispensation, imply that God's plan can be defeated by men so that God is forced to change that plan to fit altered circumstances. How can such a position escape the charge that it dishonors the Father who sees the end from the beginning and never changes His mind?

Possibly one of the most incongruous features of the theory held by many premillennialists, is the separation of the hosts of God's people during the millennium into several separate groups. According to the view held by many premillennialists, the raptured church with glorified bodies, stays somewhere in the sky while the millennium is held on the earth with the center of the millennial kingdom in Palestine.[31] Partaking in the earthly millennial kingdom are Jews who apparently are saved through believing in Christ as their Messiah, yet they are said not to have glorified bodies! Some premillennialists declare that the members of the glorified church can visit the earth during the millennium.[32] In addition to these two groups, there is the group of Jewish martyrs, who were slain during the Great Tribulation,[33] and also the group of Gentile martyrs slain during the same period.[34] They are said to be raised from the dead at the close of the Tribulation period, yet neither group seems to join the glorified church,[35] though they are declared to receive glorified bodies at their resurrection. Pretribulationists are rather vague as to the status of these groups during the alleged millennium. But there are still other groups to be accounted for. There is the group of believing Jews who did not die during the tribulation, and therefore entered the millennium with natural bodies, and the group of believing Gentiles who enter the millennium with natural bodies, having believed the "gospel of the kingdom," but not having been martyred during the tribulation. Now some of these latter groups seem to die during the alleged millennium, but it is far from clear what happens to their bodies after that time.

Thus according to these pretribulationists the body of God's people would seem to be divided during the millennium into the following groups: (1) the church with glorified bodies dwelling in the sky.[36] (2) The glorified Jewish group of believers who were martyred during the tribulation.[37] (3) The group of Gentile tribulation "saints" who are said to be raised at the close of the tribulation period but who do not join the church in the skies.[38] (4) The believing Jews who enter the millennium in natural bodies.[39]   (5) The believing Gentiles who enter the millennium in natural bodies.[40]   (6) The Jewish believers who die during the millennium.[41]   (7) The Gentile believers who die during the millennium.[42]   Doubtless many pretribulationists will be startled to face this array of different groups, for they do not usually catalog the different groups in such a way, yet their position would seem to justify such a bald analysis.

It would be unfair to charge all premillennialists with holding such positions, but the fact of the matter is that many premillennialists have never seriously attempted to correlate the different parts of their theory. The different parts of their theory have been held independently and they have never seriously faced the logical implications of the separate parts, or attempted to compare the contradictory implications. Too often the attitude of many premillennialists towards these points is hazy and nebulous in the extreme.

One of the inexplicable questions that arises in the mind of a non-premillennialist when one examines the theory of premillennialism which holds that the Jewish kingdom will be restored and be supreme during the alleged millennium, is why there should be so much enthusiasm on the part of a Gentile Christian, for a theory which holds that the church will not be present on the earth during the alleged millennium? If, as they claim, the church will be up in the skies during that period while the Jews reign on earth, why should a Gentile believer today "bleed and die," for a millennium in which he will have no direct or important concern?

The more one studies the complexities and details of the theories which seek to reconcile all the literal interpretations of the Old Testament prophecies with the literal interpretations of the words of Christ and the apostles in the New Testament, the greater is one's relief when one turns to the simple teachings of the Word of God. If one follows the New Testament leadings as to the interpretation of the Old Testament prophecies, the whole picture of the "last things" as taught in the Word of God seems so simple and easy to understand, that one is amazed at the complex theories of many modern commentators. The Bible plainly teaches that Christ is coming again, in the words of the Apostle's Creed, "to judge the quick and the dead," (II Tim. 4:1). Praise God when one becomes a Christian; that is the end of distinctions of race, and when we are raptured to meet our blessed Saviour, we won't be asked whether we are Jews or Gentiles, for in the words of the Apostle Paul, "There can be neither Jew nor Greek . . . for ye are one in Christ Jesus!"

Chapter XVI

CONCLUSION

IN our examination of the Scriptural teaching about "last things," we have seen that the general teaching of the New Testament is that our Saviour has promised to return to the earth at the end of the present dispensation in the same personal, visible way in which He ascended. He will come in power, with all the holy angels and all the souls of the redeemed hosts who have gone to be with Him in the past centuries. He will come in the Shekinah glory, the symbol of God dwelling among men. Before He comes, the forces of evil under the leadership of Satan and the personal anti-Christ will gather unbelieving nations into a great confederation to make war against the living hosts of God's elect church. They will institute a great tribulation against Christians, and there will be a multitude who will seal their faith with their blood. At the darkest hour, when it looks as though Satan and his hosts are triumphant, there will be heard the sound of the heavenly trumpet, the dead bodies of both the saved and the unsaved will rise from their graves, the souls of believers will enter their glorified bodies, join the transfigured hosts of God's people who have been alive on the earth, and together they will rise to meet the Lord in the air. The Lord, His train of angels, and redeemed Christians with the Old Testament saints will then descend to earth to judge the world. All unbelievers will be sent to hell, and a new heaven and new earth will follow after the present universe perishes in fire. Then with the conquering of all the enemies of Christ, He turns over the control to the Father and the eternal kingdom of God is set up in the world and in Heaven. In brief, this is the picture of the future that one gets from a study of the New Testament. The so-called millennial reign of Revelation 20, instead of being in the future, is in the present, with living believers reigning with Christ on the earth, while the souls of believers who have gone before, reign with Christ in Heaven.

We recognize that this picture of the future is in contrast to the literal interpretation of the prophecies of the Old Testament. We believe that the prophecies of the Old Testament were intended to picture the future in symbolic language, under the only religious symbolism that the people of that time would have understood, namely a picture of a restored theocracy, with the Holy City as the capital, and the temple with the sacrificial system as the center of all religious worship. That symbolism is full of spiritual teaching for us today, but is not intended to teach a literal restoration of the old theocracy. The New Testament gives us the key to the interpretation of those Old Testament prophecies, and shows us that the church is the heir to all the promises to the children of Abraham. The true Israelites today are only those of the *faith* of Abraham, whether the blood of Abraham flows in their veins or not. The true Zion of God is the people of God of the Old and New Testament dispensations, united in one stream. There are Jewish elements in that stream, and there are Gentile elements in it, but it is one elect people, and apart from that church today, the invisible church of the living God, believing in Christ as the Saviour who bore their sins on the cross, there is no salvation and there will be no salvation in the future. Any Jews who are to be saved must become Christians, and in the end of the age, we believe that the whole of the Israelitish people who are living at that time *will* become Christians, "when they look on Him whom they have pierced." But when they become Christian, their racial strains are merged in the Christian stream, and they are neither "Jew nor Gentile," but Christians on an equal standing with all other Christian Gentiles.

The great error of our premillennial brethren is that they have neglected to correlate the implications of different parts of their theory with the rest of Scripture, and so to see the contradictions involved thereby. In summing up, let us note a few of these contradictions from the premillennial point of view.

1. A literal interpretation of the Old Testament prophecies demands that there shall be a restoration of a Jewish Kingdom in Palestine with Jerusalem as capital, and the Jews in positions of authority over the kingdom. The literal interpretation of the alleged millennium of Rev. 20, would demand that tribulation martyrs, and all who do not worship the beast or have his mark on their forehead or on their hand, shall reign in that kingdom.

2. A literal interpretation of the prophecies of the Old Testament would demand that the temple and the whole temple ritual must be restored, including circumcision. The New Testament teaches that Christ has done away with that ritual, including sacrifice and circumcision.

3. A literal interpretation of the prophecies of the Old Testament demands that in the kingdom there shall be deaths and births during the millennium, but Jesus said that there will be no deaths, and no marriages in "that age," which follows the resurrection of the righteous.

4. A literal interpretation of Rev. 20 as applying to a future millennium demands that there will be wicked men on earth at the latter part of the millennium, but according to Matthew 25, all the wicked are sent to hell at the beginning of the alleged millennium and there will be no births during the millennium according to Jesus, for there is no marriage in "that age."

5. A literal interpretation of Rev. 20 demands that the battle of Gog and Magog shall be at the close of the millennium, while in Ezekiel 38 and 39 Gog and Magog are destroyed at the beginning of the kingdom.

These are a few of the most glaring contradictions that arise from a study of the implications of the premillennial theory. All of them are resolved if we interpret the prophecies as teaching spiritual truths in symbolic language, under the religious symbolism of the age in which the prophecies were written. By eliminating the alleged millennium, putting the two resurrections into one, the different judgments into one, and declaring that when Christ comes He comes to end this age and judge the world, we get rid of all the difficulties that beset both premillennialism and postmillennialism.

At any rate, as we said in the opening chapter, though we believe that the premillennialists are wrong, we believe we should work in cooperation with them in the church today, for our programs for Christian activity are the same until Christ comes in the clouds, and then we will know anyway which one is right. We therefore appeal to them to forget our differences and treat each other as fellow warriors in the battle against the forces of evil, rejoicing in our common hope in the coming of our Lord and Saviour.

Notes

❦

Index of Bible References

❦

General Index

NOTES

(1) C.H.M., "Papers on the Lord's Coming," p. 23, 31-32, 45.
   W. Trotter: "Plain Papers on Prophetic Subjects," p. 22. 288, 527, 557.
   Feinberg: "Premillennialism or Amillennialism," 121ff.
   Reese, "The Approaching Advent of Christ," p. 24.
   Munhall, p. 118.
   Haldeman, p. 297.

(2) Feinberg: Same, p. 122-124.
   Munhall, p. 100.
   R. A. Torrey, "The Return of the Lord Jesus," p. 64.
   F. C. Ottman, p. 410-412.

(3) C. H. M., Same, p. 17-18.
   Haldeman, p. 313.
   Wm. Kelly, "Second Coming," p. 171-172.
   J. N. Darby, "Second Coming," p. 44-45.
   Others hold that the rapture will be a public rapture, e.g. Sir Robert
      Anderson, R. A. Torrey.

(4) Seiss, Pember, Hudson Taylor, D. M. Panton: "Rapture."

(5) Reese, "Approaching Advent of Christ," p. 25-26.
   Feinberg, p. 125ff., 130.
   Munhall, p. 118.
   Torrey, p. 118.
   Torrey, "What the Bible Teaches," p. 221.
   Gaebelein, "The Work of Christ," p. 107.

(6) Scofield: "Bible Correspondence Course," p. 112-113.
   Wm. Kelly, "Christ's Coming Again," p. 99.

(7) C. H. M., "Papers on the Lord's Coming," p. 23, 31-32, 45.
   Trotter, "Plain Papers on Prophetic Subjects," p. 288.
   Kelly "Revelation," 236.

(8) Reese, Same, p. 24, 25.
     Feinberg, p. 130.
     David L. Cooper, "Messiah: His First Coming Scheduled," p. 489.
     Ford C. Ottman, "The Unfolding of the Ages," p. 185, 298.
     Darby, "Synopsis."
     Gaebelein, "Hath God."
     Trotter, "Plain papers on Prophetic Subjects," chapters on "The Spared Remnant," and "The Martyred Remnant."

(9) Reese, Same, p. 24.

(10) Feinberg, p. 130.

(11) Feinberg, p. 143.
     Reese, p. 26.

(12) F. C. Ottman, "The Unfolding of the Ages," p. 187.

(13) F. C. Ottman, p. 187.

(14) F. C. Ottman, p. xxv, 114.

(15) F. C. Ottman, p. 116.

(16) F. C. Ottman, p. 186, 264.

(17) F. C. Ottman, p. 193-194, 116.

(18) I. M. Haldeman, "The Coming of Christ," p. 253.

(19) F. C. Ottman, p. 116.
     Torrey, "What the Bible Teaches," p. 298.

(20) R. A. Torrey, "What the Bible Teaches," p. 207.
     A. C. Gaebelein, "The Return of the Lord," p. 118.

(21) F. C. Ottman, p. 114.

(22) Gaebelein, "The Work of Christ," p. 116, 117.

(23) F. C. Ottman, p. 189.
     Gaebelein, "Work of Christ," p. 117.

(24) Gaebelein, "The Return of the Lord," p. 108.

(25) Feinberg, "Premillennialism or Amillennialism," p. 122-123.
     Gaebelein, "Return of the Lord," p. 118.

(26) Feinberg, p. 121, 144.
     L. W. Munhall, "The Lord's Return," p. 96ff.
     Haldeman, "The Coming of Christ," p. 279.
     J. W. Kemp, "The Two Resurrections" in "Christ and Glory," p. 176ff.

(27) Ottman, p. 436.
George Soltau, "Plan of the Ages," p. 43.

(28) D. L. Cooper, "Messiah, His First Coming Scheduled," p. 490.
Torrey, "What the Bible Teaches," p. 211, 213.
James M. Gray "Christ the Judge," in "Christ and Glory," p. 204.

(29) Ottman, "Imperialism and Christ," p. 267.

(30) Feinberg, p. 84ff.

(31) Ottman, p. 193-194, 116.

(32) Ottman, p. 193-194, 116.

(33) Reese, p. 26.

(34) Reese, p. 26.

(35) Reese, p. 26.

(36) Ottman, p. 193-194, 116.

(37) Reese, p. 26.

(38) Reese, p. 26.

(39) A. J. Gordon, "Ecce Venit," p. 296.

(40) Ottman, p. 187.

(41) A. J. Gordon, "Ecce Venit," p. 309.

(42) Gordon, Same, p. 309.

INDEX OF BIBLE REFERENCES

GENERAL INDEX

157